Searching the
SCRIPTURES

FIND THE NOURISHMENT
YOUR SOUL NEEDS

CHARLES R.
SWINDOLL

TYNDALE
MOMENTUM™

*The nonfiction imprint of
Tyndale House Publishers, Inc.*

Visit Tyndale online at www.tyndale.com.

Visit Tyndale Momentum online at www.tyndalemomentum.com.

TYNDALE, Tyndale Momentum, and Tyndale's quill logo are registered trademarks of Tyndale House Publishers, Inc. The Tyndale Momentum logo is a trademark of Tyndale House Publishers, Inc. Tyndale Momentum is the nonfiction imprint of Tyndale House Publishers, Inc., Carol Stream, Illinois.

Searching the Scriptures: Find the Nourishment Your Soul Needs

Designed by Ron Kaufmann

Edited by Stephanie Rische

Published in association with Yates & Yates, LLP (www.yates2.com).

For information about special discounts for bulk purchases, please contact Tyndale House Publishers at csresponse@tyndale.com, or call 1-800-323-9400.

Library of Congress Cataloging-in-Publication Data
Names: Swindoll, Charles R., author.
Title: Searching the scriptures : find the nourishment your soul needs / Charles R. Swindoll.
Description: Carol Stream, IL : Tyndale House Publishers, Inc., 2016. | Includes bibliographical references.
Identifiers: LCCN 2016021428 | ISBN 9781414380650 (hc)
Subjects: LCSH: Bible—Hermeneutics.
Classification: LCC BS476 .S95 2016 | DDC 220.6—dc23 LC record available at https://lccn.loc.gov/2016021428

ISBN 978-1-4143-8066-7 (Softcover)

Printed in the United States of America

23 22 21 20 19 18 17
7   6   5   4   3   2   1a

It is with genuine delight and profound feelings of gratitude that I dedicate this book to my longtime friend, mentor, and former professor

DR. HOWARD G. HENDRICKS.

We met in the fall of 1959 as I began my studies at Dallas Theological Seminary. He taught me many of the principles and techniques that I have included in this book. His passion to search the Scriptures has stayed with me throughout my ministry. His instruction has guided me all these years in preparing and delivering the truths of the Word of God to those who hunger for spiritual nourishment. Most important, these techniques have transformed my own life.

Following Dr. Hendricks's death on February 20, 2013, I determined to prolong the memory of his life by sharing with others what he faithfully invested in me so many years ago. This book has been written in his honor.

CONTENTS

INTRODUCTION
A Testimony from the Chef

FOR MORE THAN SIXTY YEARS I have cultivated a love for the Bible and have pursued an understanding of it. My purpose in writing this book is to help you do the same.

First, I'd like to offer an explanation of how this love affair started. As early as my late teens, I was drawn to the truths of God's Word and captivated by its wisdom. My interest in the Bible can be traced in large part to the fact that I was reared by a mother and a father who believed in God and respected the Scriptures. They used the Bible's counsel as a guideline for our home, often quoting from its pages as my older brother, Orville; my older sister, Luci; and I were growing up. It was back then that the Bible first began to make sense to me.

Because scriptural truth served as our domestic foundation, ours was a home where respect for authority was expected and lovingly enforced. At the same time, my parents allowed for open discussion and gave us the freedom to speak our minds. Disagreements in our home didn't fester and lead to unending arguments; rather, they were resolved quickly and correctly, just as the Bible teaches. Ours was not an uptight, frowning family marked by harsh demands or mindless rules and regulations. On the contrary, while my parents honored, taught, and respected the Bible, they also encouraged lighthearted fun. In our home, laughter was loud and frequent, and the sounds of music—both vocal and instrumental—were heard every day. In that happy, balanced setting, I never felt abused or exploited by overbearing, obsessive parents who hammered us children with a long list of legalistic requirements underscored by Bible verses yanked out of context. On the contrary, grace flowed often and freely.

Having grown up in that type of environment, I was interested in cultivating a relationship with a woman who had standards similar to mine. I longed to find a life partner who loved the Lord and His Word; who found delight in free-flowing, in-depth conversation; who enjoyed music, lots of good humor, and laughter; and who was committed to deepening her knowledge of scriptural truth. When Cynthia and I met, I quickly realized that she was the one, which led to our being engaged—in one week(!)—and marrying eighteen months later. Throughout our courtship, we found a mutual interest in digging into the Scriptures. We regularly attended Bible studies together in order to establish our home on the rock-solid foundation of the Bible.

Less than two years after we married, my hitch in the Marine Corps resulted in my spending more than sixteen months apart from my wife on the Japanese island of Okinawa. Even there, I intensified my study of the Bible. Thanks to a man named Bob Newkirk, a representative of the Navigators serving on the island, I dug deeper into my understanding of God's Word, which included an extensive Scripture-memory program and a weekly Bible study with others who were serving in various branches of the military. As a result, it became clear to me that I should pursue an even deeper study of Scripture at a seminary, with a view toward entering full-time ministry.

This calling came as an unexpected surprise to me since it

represented a complete change of direction in my career. Cynthia was delighted with the decision. Within weeks after my discharge from the Marine Corps, in the summer of 1959, we were on our way to Dallas Theological Seminary (DTS). We towed a small U-Haul trailer full of our belongings, smiling from ear to ear as we anticipated the excitement of learning and growing together. I cannot describe the sheer delight within me, knowing that my love for God would be enlarged and deepened, my mind would be stretched and challenged as never before, and my hunger for a deeper understanding of the Scriptures would begin to be satisfied. The next four years were nothing short of life changing.

It was during that time that I became acquainted with Dr. Howard G. Hendricks, who was the professor for my major and chair of the Department of Christian Education. While I took every subject he taught during those years of study, the one that proved most beneficial was his best-known course, at the time titled Bible Study Methods. Even though I had been a student of the Bible since my late-teen years, I began to realize how incomplete and inadequate my approach to the Scriptures had been. Though I had slowly grown in my knowledge of God's Word over the previous years, I didn't have a consistent method of studying those truths and interpreting them—one that would lead to insightful and accurate applications of the Scriptures. While I had been sincere and committed during those earlier years, my method of searching the Scriptures lacked a systematic, trustworthy approach. Thanks to what I learned in this magnificent course of study from "Prof" Hendricks at Dallas Theological Seminary, I finally discovered how to engage in a meaningful and reliable process of searching the Scriptures.

When my wife witnessed my excitement as I shared those principles with her, she invited Dr. Hendricks to teach them to the spouses of the seminary students as well. She organized a wives' fellowship that gathered one evening each week, during which he taught them the same techniques he'd been teaching us. A contagious spirit of excitement swept across our campus as husbands and wives were involved in their own study of the Bible, many of them for the first time in their married lives.

The principles Cynthia and I learned in my early years of study at DTS are the same principles I have used since entering the ministry in 1963. Not a week passes without my returning to those tried-and-true guidelines I imbibed decades ago. To this day, I have not delivered a sermon, conducted a teaching session, released a broadcast or podcast, or given even a brief devotional without first putting those principles to use.

For me, opening up God's Word became like a banquet feast. What I learned from Prof Hendricks became nourishment for my soul. Because these principles have served me so well for more than fifty years of ministry, I want to pass them on to others—*including you*—on the pages of this book. As a result of your learning them and putting them into practice, you, too, can know the fulfillment of opening the pages of your Bible without feeling fearful or intimidated. You, too, can share confidently with others what you glean from your study of the Scriptures. If you are a minister of the gospel, an evangelist, a missionary, or one who teaches God's Word in any other capacity, you can be certain that what you are communicating is in keeping with what God has written. You can experience the joy of personal discovery, as well as the great satisfaction of helping others gain an understanding of God's truth.

The process of getting these principles into your head and heart is like passing a baton in a relay. Years ago I was handed these magnificent insights from one who modeled them, and it is now my delight to pass the baton from my hand to yours. This relay has been going on for centuries. The aging missionary Paul wrote these words to Timothy, his younger friend who was shepherding a church in ancient Ephesus: "Now teach these truths to other trustworthy people who will be able to pass them on to others" (2 Timothy 2:2). By the time you finish reading these pages, you will be well equipped to search the Scriptures on your own and well prepared to pass on the baton to others with great joy and quiet confidence.

Before we begin, I need to express my profound gratitude to my very capable colleague and keen-eyed editor, Rhome Dyck. He has faithfully worked alongside me from the starting blocks to the finish line. His creative mind and skillful hands have been of inestimable value in assisting me as we have honed ideas, shaped those thoughts into words, carefully planned the interior design, and then pulled everything together to create this book. My gratitude for this gifted man knows no bounds.

Chuck Swindoll
FRISCO, TEXAS

Finding the Food

CHAPTER I

SURVEYING THE SHELVES

Understanding the Basic Story of the Bible

PEOPLE ARE FRUSTRATED. Maybe you are one of them.

Here's the deal. You pick up a Bible, and you've got this big, thick book with thin pages and tiny print. You've been told that it's the all-time bestseller, that thousands—more like millions—of people have had their lives changed or their marriages transformed by what is written there. But as hard as you try, you still can't make heads or tails of any of it! Others may have been helped and comforted, but you're stumped. As a matter of fact, you're completely confused. As much as you want to understand all this, none of it makes sense.

What's wrong? What's missing? Even though you are fairly intelligent and are dedicated to going deeper with God's Word, why can't you get excited about it?

If the Bible were a gourmet meal, you'd certainly find yourself starving to death. Just as you need to know your way around the kitchen if you want to learn to cook, you need to know the basic structure of the Bible and the main staples of the nourishment it provides. You'll also want to discover some of the unique flavors God's Word offers. That's what we'll try to do in this chapter. We'll first look at how the Bible is put together. Then we'll discover why we should take time to study it and learn what it can teach us. By breaking Scripture down into smaller sections, we'll get a better handle on what God is saying to us. Along the way, we will also begin to see the consistency, importance, and beauty of God's message. So let's get started!

AN OVERVIEW OF THE BIBLE

The first thing we need to know is that the Bible includes a total of sixty-six individual books. Some of these books are personal letters, some are songs, and others are like journals or diaries; and then there are law codes and histories. The words of the Bible were breathed by God and recorded by approximately forty human authors over a period of approximately 1,500 years. As Paul explains to his protégé Timothy, "All Scripture is inspired by God and is useful to teach us what is true and to make us realize what is wrong in our lives. It corrects us when we are wrong and teaches us to do what is right" (2 Timothy 3:16).

The Bible is divided into two major sections: the Old Testament, which anticipates the coming of Jesus, the Messiah; and the New Testament, which presents Jesus as the Messiah and explains His ministry and purpose.

One surprising aspect of Scripture is that the books don't appear in chronological order. No wonder so many people are frustrated when they try to understand the Bible!

It's helpful to remember this: the Bible is put together much like a newspaper. Think of the way a newspaper is laid out. All the news stories are placed in one section, the sports reports and statistics are put in another section, the business or lifestyle stories are grouped together in yet another section, and the want ads are in another.

Likewise, in the Bible, the Old Testament begins with the books of ancient history—from Genesis to Esther. Following that section, the books of poetry appear together—from Job to Song of Solomon. Finally, in the last part of the Old Testament, we come to the books of prophecy—from Isaiah to Malachi. These three major sections representing three types of literature comprise the thirty-nine books of the Old Testament. The New Testament is set up in a similar way. The Gospels include the books of Matthew, Mark, Luke, and John and tell the Good News of Jesus' life, death, and resurrection. Acts is a book of history, and it covers the establishment of the church. Then come all the letters, which are usually divided into the letters of Paul (Romans through Philemon), and the general letters (Hebrews through Jude). Finally there's Revelation, which is a book of prophecy.

As we begin our brief journey through Scripture, we are able to see that God's Word wasn't designed to be just a pretty book sitting on a coffee table. Rather, we might think of the Bible as a delicious meal—in fact, as a feast meant to be enjoyed and savored. Each time we are hungry deep in our souls, we need to return to the Scriptures for our spiritual sustenance. Interestingly, the more we learn and grow from searching the Scriptures on our own, the better equipped we will be to teach others those tasty truths.

TYPES OF BOOKS IN THE BIBLE	
The Old Testament	**The New Testament**
Books of History	*The Gospels*
Genesis–Esther	Matthew–John
Books of Poetry	*Book of History*
Job–Song of Solomon	Acts
Books of Prophecy	*The Letters*
Isaiah–Malachi	Romans–Jude
	Book of Prophecy
	Revelation

THE OLD TESTAMENT
The Books of History

The first course of our literary banquet is served to us in the first section of the Old Testament. Often this historical section of Scripture is called *narrative* because God is communicating His Word as a grand story. However, since the first five books of the Bible contain the Ten Commandments and the laws for Israel to follow, they are most frequently referred to as the Law. The story begins in Genesis 1 with God creating all things. The crown jewel of His creation? You guessed it: Adam and Eve, who bore their Creator's image. Living in perfect communion with God, Adam and Eve were given the opportunity to obey their Creator. But barely into the story, in Genesis 3, they rebelled against and disobeyed God's command. Their sin fractured their relationship with their holy God.

From this point on in Scripture, we witness again and again the horrific results of sin. At the same time, we observe the grace and forgiveness of God, who carefully unfolds His plan to redeem His creation. In Genesis 12, God chooses Abram (who later becomes Abraham) and his wife, Sarai (Sarah), to be the parents of a special nation. Eventually this nation becomes known as Israel. Through Abraham and his offspring, all the families of the earth will be blessed. What an important and wonderful promise!

The rest of Genesis tells the fascinating stories of Abraham and the next three generations. Over time they grew into a large family and wound up in Egypt because of a famine. With a flip of the page, the book of Exodus continues the story four hundred years later, with Abraham's family having been blessed by God and having grown into a nation made up of twelve tribes. Fearing their potential power, the Egyptians enslaved the Israelites. When the Israelites cried out to God for relief from unfair and excruciating labor, He responded by raising up Moses to deliver His people from Egypt and to bring them to His special Promised Land.

The narrative continues, and on the way to the Promised Land, God gave the Israelites His law to follow and live by. These codes explain how God's people are to enjoy a loving relationship with Him and each other. When the twelve tribes finally arrived at the doorstep of the Promised Land, however, they ultimately didn't trust God to deliver them. The Promised Land was occupied by the formidable Canaanites, whom the Israelites assumed were impossible to conquer. Fear eclipsed faith. Consequently, that unbelieving generation was left to die off as they wandered in the desert for forty long years. Much of that wandering is covered in the last part of Exodus and through the book of Numbers.

The book of Deuteronomy is actually a message to the grown children of the unbelieving generation that died in the desert. God called Moses to repeat and underscore His laws to this new generation. The challenge to know and teach God's Word is clear:

These are the commands, decrees, and regulations that the Lord your God commanded me to teach you. You must obey them in the land you are about to enter and occupy, and you and your children and grandchildren must fear the Lord your God as long as you live. If you obey all his decrees and commands, you will enjoy a long life. Listen closely, Israel, and be careful to obey. Then all will go well with you, and you will have many children in the land flowing with milk and honey, just as the Lord, the God of your ancestors, promised you.

Listen, O Israel! The Lord is our God, the Lord alone. And you must love the Lord your God with all your heart, all your soul, and all your strength. And you must commit yourselves wholeheartedly to these commands that I am giving you today. Repeat them again and again to your children. Talk about them when you are at home and when

you are on the road, when you are going to bed and when
you are getting up. Tie them to your hands and wear them
on your forehead as reminders. Write them on the doorposts
of your house and on your gates.

DEUTERONOMY 6:1-9

Notice from those words that Moses was charged with *teaching* the
Israelites to obey God's Word. Also note that learning God's Word
creates results—in this case, obedience. Furthermore, God told the
people that obedience would allow them to *enjoy a long life*. These
first few sentences of Deuteronomy 6 are saying, in summary, that
obedience to God's Word results in God's blessing.

However, obeying God isn't automatic; it isn't accomplished by
simply knowing His instruction. We learn here that wholeheartedly
loving our great God includes teaching and explaining His Word
to others. So what is the point God is communicating here? That
parents have the responsibility to teach and remind their children
of God's truths. This ancient command is to be obeyed today, just
as when it was first given. Generation after generation is to learn,
obey, and teach the truths of the Lord. Timeless passages like this
apply to all generations—including our own.

This is a good time to point out that the study of God's Word
is for everyone. While there is a specific role for the pastor-teacher,
God doesn't limit the explanation of His Word to certain special-
ists. Rather, God's Word is to be learned, applied, obeyed, and
passed on and on and on. Everyday people, including parents who
teach their kids, are all part of His plan. Searching the Scriptures
isn't restricted to any specialized group—the Scriptures are acces-
sible to anyone and everyone.

By the way, the diligent study of God's Word isn't mentioned
only in the book of Deuteronomy. It's a theme you'll find repeated
throughout the Bible.

Now let's get back to the biblical story. The grand narrative progresses as God leads the new generation to conquer the Promised Land under Joshua's leadership. But sadly, once the twelve tribes settled in the land, they struggled to faithfully obey their God. That led to a period when Israel was ruled by judges whom God raised up. God would deliver His people from their enemies only to have the people repeatedly fall into sin again. It was a wicked, tragic cycle! Eventually, out of rebellion against God, the people asked God for a human king so they could be like the pagan nations around them. He gave them their request, but they lived to regret it.

The Books of Poetry

The next part of the Bible's story takes us into the beginning of the kingdom of Israel, first under King Saul, then King David, and finally King Solomon. This collection of books is sometimes called *wisdom literature*, because it was written to impart God's wisdom to those who believe and obey God's Word.

The book of Proverbs is one of the books of poetry in the Old Testament. Written and collected mostly by Solomon, Proverbs explains and extols wise behavior in the eyes of the Lord. Consider the beginning of chapter 2:

> My child, listen to what I say,
> and treasure my commands.
> Tune your ears to wisdom,
> and concentrate on understanding.
> Cry out for insight,
> and ask for understanding.
> Search for them as you would for silver;
> seek them like hidden treasures.
> Then you will understand what it means to fear the Lord,
> and you will gain knowledge of God.

For the Lord grants wisdom!
　　From his mouth come knowledge and understanding.
He grants a treasure of common sense to the honest.
　　He is a shield to those who walk with integrity.
He guards the paths of the just
　　and protects those who are faithful to him.

Then you will understand what is right, just, and fair,
　　and you will find the right way to go.

PROVERBS 2:1-9

In this passage, God is reminding us to hear and study and obey His instructions. Notice the diligence involved in the study of God's Word: we are to search for it as one would search for hidden treasure. I can vividly remember the determination and diligence with which I dug into the pages of the Bible when I got serious about my faith while serving in the Marines on the island of Okinawa. What treasures I found as I searched the Scriptures! I dug even deeper when I went to seminary.

Proverbs 2 explains what is gained from the study of Scripture: wisdom to find the right course of action for one's life. The Bible, as God's inerrant Word, gives us the insight we need. This is why people who have learned to study the Scriptures are some of the most joyful, peaceful people on the planet. It takes some effort to learn how to consistently draw truth from the Bible, but it is well worth the effort. As we get into the process involved in searching the Scriptures later in this book, you will discover how beneficial such study can be.

The Books of Prophecy
God's persistent call to study His Word isn't always given as a positive command. Sometimes He confronts His people with the sin of ignoring Him and His commands. This is often seen in the books

of the prophets, which are contained in the third and final section of the Old Testament. Those prophets were a strong-hearted, tough-minded bunch!

KINGS OF ISRAEL

The United Kingdom

Saul

David

Solomon

The Divided Kingdom

Kings of Israel	Kings of Judah
Jeroboam I	Rehoboam
Nadab	Abijah/Abijam
Baasha	Asa
Elah	Jehoshaphat
Zimri	Jehoram/Joram
Omri	Ahaziah/Jehoahaz
Ahab	Athaliah (queen)
Ahaziah	Joash/Jehoash
Joram/Jehoram	Amaziah
Jehu	Uzziah
Jehoahaz	Jotham
Joash/Jehoash	Ahaz
Jeroboam II	Hezekiah
Zechariah	Manasseh
Shallum	Amon
Menahem	Josiah
Pekahiah	Jehoahaz
Pekah	Jehoiakim
Hoshea	Jehoiachin/Jeconiah
	Zedekiah

The books from Isaiah to Daniel make up the five *Major Prophets* in the Old Testament. They are called Major Prophets simply because their writings are longer. Then there are twelve *Minor Prophets* who wrote shorter books: Hosea through Malachi. A prophet's job was to speak for God. He communicated God's clear, firm, and often confrontational message to direct the reigning king and the people in the ways of the Lord. In one sense, this was the highest office in the land of Israel—even more important than the king. However, the prophets were often ignored, mocked, ridiculed, and even put to death by the kings or the people.

After the first three kings of Israel (Saul, David, and Solomon), the kingdom split over the issue of taxes. The northern ten tribes united and kept the name *Israel*. The southern two tribes joined forces under the name *Judah*. This period of the divided kingdom lasted until the end of the Old Testament. (Note that it's always a good idea to pay close attention when reading in 1 and 2 Kings and 1 and 2 Chronicles, as sometimes the writer is addressing events in the northern kingdom and other times, the southern kingdom.)

Each kingdom had its own kings. God raised up prophets during this time to speak to the kings and the people. Here are three simple points to remember about the role of a prophet:

> As a mouthpiece for God, prophets were primarily concerned with restoring the relationship between God and His people.

> Prophets constantly called for repentance and warned of impending judgment.

> Prophets offered a message of hope as they foretold of a future when God would restore His people.

Despite the warnings from the prophets, however, no less than twenty successive kings ignored the word of the Lord, and judgment came for the northern ten tribes. In 722 BC, the powerful nation of Assyria attacked and captured the kingdom of Israel and integrated the nation into its own wicked empire.

KEY DATES IN ISRAEL'S HISTORY

931BC	722BC	586BC		4BC

931 BC The kingdom divides after Solomon's death.
722 BC Assyria captures and exiles the northern kingdom (Israel).
586 BC Babylon destroys Jerusalem and exiles the southern kingdom (Judah) for seventy years.
4 BC (?) Jesus is born in Bethlehem.

The southern kingdom didn't fare much better. The nation had an occasional righteous king, but for the most part, it, too, was marked by disobedience. Approximately 150 years after the northern kingdom fell to Assyria, the southern kingdom was attacked by Babylon and taken into exile in 586 BC. Like the Assyrians, the Babylonians were a ruthless, cutthroat people. They destroyed everything in their way, including the capital city of Jerusalem, its walls, and the Temple that Solomon had built for God.

The prophet Jeremiah lived in the tumultuous days leading up to Judah's Babylonian exile. God's message through him is an example of a judgment from the Lord that was typical of the prophets. The Lord's words were sharp, as His people continued to ignore Him:

"My people are foolish
and do not know me," says the LORD.
"They are stupid children
who have no understanding.
They are clever enough at doing wrong,
but they have no idea how to do right!"

JEREMIAH 4:22

How's that for telling it like it is? God's prophets didn't hold back; they declared truth without fear.

This judgment against disobedience serves as an important reminder to all people, including us today. God has made Himself known through His Book, the Bible. We are foolish if we don't make a careful study of His Word. Here's a good motto to remember: no study, no stability. There is no shortcut to maturity. It comes slowly but surely to those who search the Scriptures.

The disobedience of the people of Judah ultimately led to their exile in Babylon. However, God wasn't silent. He continued to raise up various prophets such as Daniel and Ezekiel to call the people to repent of their sins. Those prophets also predicted a coming Messiah, who would ultimately save Israel from their sin.

After seventy grueling, lonely years of captivity, the Persian Empire under King Cyrus conquered the Babylonian Empire and let the captives return to their homeland. But many captives had become comfortable in Babylon and Persia, so less than half the people returned to the Promised Land. The Old Testament closes with Israel as a mere shadow of its former self. The remnants were struggling to reestablish themselves after rebuilding the protective walls of Jerusalem and a very modest version of Solomon's Temple. They longed for their coming Messiah to restore their land.

The story of the rebuilding of Jerusalem is told in the historical books of the Old Testament Ezra and Nehemiah, as well as through the prophets. This is why readers of the Bible can get confused when reading about the events that occurred during the time of the divided kingdom. There are two sets of kings, one in the north and one in the south, and there are at least two books where the story is being explained—the historical narrative and the account through the mouth of God's reigning prophet. Small wonder so many people stop reading through their Bibles when they come to the era of the two kingdoms!

Now that the basic plot of the Old Testament has been laid out for you, it's like having a recipe for the main dish you're about to prepare. You can familiarize yourself with the ingredients and the steps needed so you can get the full nourishment and enjoyment from the meal. The study of God's Word is neither optional nor occasional. It is the source of wisdom, knowledge, and understanding for daily living—both in ancient times and today. The longer you search the Scriptures, the more you'll see how relevant the Bible is. It is as timeless as it is true.

THE NEW TESTAMENT
The Four Gospels

Let's press on in our scriptural banquet. Some four hundred years after Malachi, the last prophet of the Old Testament, we come to our second course: the New Testament, which offers the long-awaited hope promised by the prophets of God. The first four books of the New Testament—Matthew, Mark, Luke, and John—are often referred to as the *Gospels*. *Gospel* is a term that simply means "good news." The good news presented in these four books is that Jesus is the long-awaited Messiah. Each of the four books tells the story of the life, death, and resurrection of Jesus. Each writer shows his particular audience how God has offered salvation to us all through His Son, Jesus.

Jesus' ministry was marked by a unique style of teaching that we need to become familiar with. He frequently taught people using *parables*, or short stories that conveyed a specific point. Consider Jesus' words at His first and most famous sermon, the Sermon on the Mount:

Anyone who listens to my teaching and follows it is wise, like a person who builds a house on solid rock. Though the rain comes in torrents and the floodwaters rise and the winds beat against that house, it won't collapse because it is built on bedrock. But anyone who hears my teaching and doesn't obey it is foolish, like a person who builds a house on sand. When the rains and floods come and the winds beat against that house, it will collapse with a mighty crash.

MATTHEW 7:24-27

The imagery in this story is clear. Listening to—and obeying—the words of Christ is equivalent to building a home on a solid, rocklike foundation. But ignoring those teachings is the same as building a house on a shaky, shifting foundation. Regardless of the foundation we've built our lives upon, all of us will face difficulties . . . and those who are not grounded in the truth of Christ's teaching "will collapse with a mighty crash."

Jesus' message is powerful and timeless. Though some words and principles of the Bible may seem intimidating at first, we can't allow that to stop us from digging in. The results of ignorance are absolutely devastating. The four passages we've looked at in this chapter offer a consistent message: studying the Bible is not only possible but doable. This habit is indispensable for life and ministry. There is no substitute! Searching the Scriptures yields a richness in life unlike anything else.

One Book of History

After the first four books in the New Testament (the Gospels), we come to a single book of history called Acts, or the Acts of the Apostles. This exciting narrative picks up the story of Jesus where the Gospels end. It begins with Christ's ascension to heaven, followed by the coming and empowering of the Holy Spirit. Acts then tells the story of the start of the church, as Jesus-followers share the good news of Jesus' death and resurrection with others, and then begin planting churches all over the known world.

The Letters of Paul

The remainder of the New Testament is made up of letters written by several of Jesus' followers who were inspired by the Holy Spirit to record reliable truths to live by. They explain the meaning of the Savior's life, death, and resurrection. The first set of letters is written by the apostle Paul, starting with Romans all the way to Philemon. Included in this group are two letters that Paul wrote to his younger friend and understudy in ministry, Timothy. The second letter to Timothy, written at the end of Paul's life, includes this charge:

> Work hard so you can present yourself to God and receive his approval. Be a good worker, one who does not need to be ashamed and who correctly explains the word of truth.
>
> 2 TIMOTHY 2:15

Paul's challenge to Timothy was to "work hard," or study, so he would be able to explain the Bible accurately. Sound familiar? Just as God said in Deuteronomy 6, learning and obeying God's Word always leads to the teaching of God's Word. Paul wanted to ensure that Timothy understood this formula as the primary goal of his ministry. That same charge is passed down to us today. Our call is to correctly explain the Scriptures to others . . . but that will require careful and diligent work on our part. The Bible does not yield its truth to lazy minds!

The General Letters

After Paul's letters, the New Testament includes various letters written by other followers of Jesus—the books of Hebrews through

Jude. Similar to Paul's letters, they call followers of Christ to lives of faithfulness, discipline, purity, and service to others. These letters help us understand the purpose and structure of the church and the ministries it is to carry out—regardless of the time or era in which the church exists.

One Book of Prophecy
The final book of the New Testament is Revelation, which offers a prophetic look at the end of human history. It tells of the glorious return of our Savior, the judgment of sin, and how Christ will make all things new.

These four sections of the New Testament—the Gospels, history, letters, and prophecy—complete our multicourse meal through all sixty-six books of the Scriptures. Hopefully you have begun to realize that searching the Scriptures not only is commanded by God but can be done, with some assistance. We can do this together. It will be my joy to help you learn the Scriptures yourself and then learn to explain God's truth to others. Are you salivating for God's Word yet?

Long before books as we know them were invented, the Bible was a collection of scrolls written on rolled-up parchment (see the insert at the back of this book). The shelves represent the categories the books of the Bible can be divided into. This is the way our Bibles are arranged today, except that the individual scrolls are now found in one large book.

As we dig into various passages in the next section, "Your Turn in the Kitchen," I hope you are working up an appetite to devour the spiritual food that we will feast upon. God's Word promises us knowledge, understanding, and wisdom for living. It's going to be a delicious meal, but as Solomon told his son and as Paul told Timothy, it's also going to take some hard work.

I am grateful to mentors such as Bob Newkirk on Okinawa,

Prof Hendricks at Dallas Seminary, Ray Stedman at Peninsula Bible
Church, and many others along the way for teaching me diligence
in the study of God's Word. The persistence they required of me has
shaped my life and ministry for more than sixty years. Now, in turn,
I want to pass the baton to you. I urge you to take hold of it.

This book will help you feast and be satisfied at the table of
Scripture. In the process, I hope you will also learn to prepare delicious meals for others. This is the meal of a lifetime, and it deserves
our best effort. Are you ready to dig in?

YOUR TURN IN THE KITCHEN

When it comes to cooking, it's not enough to read about it or watch someone else do it; you have to actually get in the kitchen, roll up your sleeves, think about how much you will enjoy fixing your own meal, and then give it your best effort! The same is true when it comes to studying the Bible. So now it's time to roll up your mental sleeves and spend some time in the Scriptures on your own. Here are a few exercises for you to try.

1. Turn to the table of contents in your Bible. Using the labels on the scrolls (see insert), divide the list of books into sections and label each section with the appropriate title (law, history, poetry, etc.). This way every time you look at the table of contents in your Bible, you will be reminded of how the books are arranged thematically.

2. In your own Bible, reread the five passages that we discussed in this chapter:

> Deuteronomy 6:1-9
> Proverbs 2:1-9
> Jeremiah 4:22
> Matthew 7:24-27
> 2 Timothy 2:15

Create a list of God's commands in the above passages.
Use the exact words from your Bible.

3. Create another list of God's commands using two additional
   passages. The first is Joshua 1:7-9, where God gives the
   leadership of Israel over to Joshua after Moses' death. The
   second passage is Ezra 7:10, where Ezra, a scribe, returns
   to Jerusalem from Babylon to lead the people.

   What can you learn about studying the Scriptures from
   these two passages?

4. There are many Scripture passages that review events from
   previous times in biblical history. When we read about
   these events slowly and carefully, we begin to understand
   and picture the overall story of the Bible. Carefully read Acts
   7:1-53, where Stephen reminds his countrymen of their
   history of unfaithfulness. In a sentence or two, summarize
   what Stephen says about each of these biblical figures:

> Abraham
> Joseph
> Moses
> Aaron
> Joshua
> David
> Solomon

5. Learning is truly mastered when we can explain what we've learned to someone else. Find a family member, a colleague, or a close friend who may be interested in what you're learning about the Bible. Tell this person why you have become excited about studying the Scriptures and why the Bible has become so important to you. Select a couple of the sections of Scripture you read earlier and read them to this person. Briefly explain what you've read, and then share some of the insights you noted in the previous questions.

CHAPTER 2

CONSIDERING TRUE NOURISHMENT

Discovering the Transforming Nature of the Bible

NO ONE CAN DENY THE IMPORTANCE of bodily nutrition. Our energy levels, our ability to cope with life's challenges, and even our mental attitudes are directly linked to the intake of the right foods eaten regularly and in proper amounts. We all know what it's like to eat an unbalanced diet or consume too many sweets or choke down too much too quickly or skip a meal altogether. Invariably, we endure any number of consequences as a result. We feel sick or light-headed, or we may become irritated, edgy, and even depressed. Sometimes we get a little shaky; in my family, we call that "getting the jitters." This is the body's way of letting us know that it's lacking sufficient nourishment. Optimal health requires optimal nutrition.

The same is true when it comes to spiritual matters. Without sufficient and regular biblical nutrition, our inner lives begin to suffer the consequences. Our souls long to be fed, nourished, and energized by the Scriptures on a regular basis. When we fail to set aside time to digest healthy spiritual food, it isn't long before the consequences start to kick in . . . and it's not a pretty sight. We start to operate out of the flesh rather than under the control of God's Spirit. We become shallow and selfish, more demanding, and less gentle. We react impatiently, rashly, and angrily. These are telltale signs of inner malnutrition.

In order to make sure our souls are properly nourished, we need to prepare nutritious spiritual meals for ourselves. But how can we do that? First, we need to evaluate what will go into a meal. What is the nutritional value of each ingredient? Delicious meals served in fine restaurants never just happen. They take time and a great deal of effort. Any meal worth eating begins with nourishing food that is fresh, clean, and carefully prepared. Chefs don't throw a bunch of things together in a haphazard manner; rather, they follow a specific recipe, paying careful attention to important details. After the food has been properly prepared, it is presented in attractive, creative ways. The result is reliable: the meal is succulent, and those who enjoy it are satisfied and grateful. Chances are good that everyone who shared the meal will return again and again.

This is precisely the pattern we need to follow when we come to the Scriptures. Before we dive into the Bible, we need to think about preparation. First, we must consider the nutritional value of studying God's Word. What will be the benefits of learning to search the Scriptures for ourselves? It's not enough to have a pastor or a teacher feed us once a week; we need to be able to prepare our own spiritual meals on a daily basis.

LONGING FOR DEEPER SATISFACTION
We've all been in a hurry at some point and grabbed fast food instead of planning and cooking a balanced meal. We barely stop to enjoy the food as we wolf it down on the go. It may satisfy our

hunger for a while, but it provides little nourishment. Spiritual fast food presents the same problem. A quick glance at a verse or two on the way out the door doesn't give us long-term growth or satisfaction. Our spiritual food needs to be carefully prepared so it will sustain us and refresh us and satisfy the deepest longings of our souls.

Have you lived long enough to realize, like the psalmist says, that ours is a parched land, where there is little to satisfy the hunger of the heart (see Psalm 63:1)? While we long to dive deep into the things of God, it's difficult to carve out time to do that in our fast-paced world. We tend to dash from one event to another, not giving much thought to what has happened or what might occur . . . or what will happen as a result of what we're doing.

A. W. Tozer aptly described this tendency toward spiritual shallowness: "May not the inadequacy of much of our spiritual experience be traced back to our habit of skipping through the corridors of the kingdom like children through the marketplace, chattering about everything, but pausing to learn the true value of nothing?"[1]

Have you been around people like that, who skim along the surface of faith? Then there's a more penetrating and important question: Is that you? Looking back over all the years that you have known Christ, is there any measurable difference in your walk, your growth, your depth? As a result of the years you've spent growing older, have you measurably grown up?

God doesn't want us to merely scratch the surface of life, unsure of why we're feeling so empty. He longs for us to dig deeper so we can find out what God may be saying to us in the middle of our busy lives.

This world offers so much in the way of distraction and entertainment—often to the point that we become numb to our need for soul nourishment. Let's pause here for a moment of self-reflection. Do you spend your days seeking to be entertained? Or have you come to the place where you prefer to think deeply, to nourish your soul with spiritual truth? It's not that I'm against entertainment. I am, however, against superficial, mindless entertainment that doesn't prompt us to think deeply and insults our intelligence.

Toward the end of Hebrews 5, the writer seems frustrated . . . or perhaps *exasperated* would be a better way to put it. He has just introduced an unusual subject: "the order of Melchizedek." Right away, if you're like most people, you wonder, *What is that all about?* But if you had lived in the first century AD and had been actively engaged in spiritual growth, you would have known all about Melchizedek. That's the point the writer is making in verse 11— that his readers weren't examples of such maturity.

> There is much more we would like to say about this, but it is difficult to explain, especially since you are spiritually dull and don't seem to listen.
>
> HEBREWS 5:11

The writer of this letter was hoping to get his readers to understand that they weren't hard of hearing; they were hard of listening! That problem wasn't confined to Christians in the early church. When the subject gets deep, do we look at our watches or our phones, wondering when the teaching time will end so we can get back to being entertained?

The writer is saying, essentially, "I have much more to say, which includes many things you need to know about your life, but I can't go there." It would be like describing CPR to a three-year-old. It's understandable that a three-year-old can't grasp the ins and outs of detailed teaching, but when someone doesn't get it as an adult, it's tragic.

Read the next verse carefully:

You have been believers so long now that you ought to be
teaching others. Instead, you need someone to teach you
again the basic things about God's word. You are like babies
who need milk and cannot eat solid food.

HEBREWS 5:12

The writer indicates that his readers have been walking with the
Lord for a number of years, like many of us. He's saying, in essence,
"By this time you ought to have enough truth under your belt
to be able to lead a class of young learners. You should be able to
help other people grasp what God is saying as you think your way
through the Scriptures. But the truth is, you're still playing with the
building blocks in the nursery. You're still looking over the ABCs of
life rather than understanding the deeper truths. You're so satisfied
with the basics that you've gotten stuck in your spiritual journey."

I've been there; I identify with those words. When Cynthia and I
were young adults, we realized that if we remained at the church we
were in, we would continue to be stunted in our growth. We weren't
being challenged to learn; we were being fed milk, like babies on
bottles. We weren't being taught to prepare our own spiritual meals.
We determined that our wisest course of action was to break free
from the tradition we'd been a part of all our lives and to seek a
church where we would be fed the nourishing meat of the Word
of God and where we'd be challenged to think deeply and begin to
grow in our faith. We did that, and oh, the difference it made!

The writer of Hebrews was concerned that his audience hadn't
made the decision to grow up in their faith. They were willing to
remain stuck in the nursery. Look at how verse 12 ends:

You are like babies who need milk and cannot eat solid food.

HEBREWS 5:12

Milk is a wonderful thing when it's placed in the mouth of a tiny newborn. As the little one sucks contentedly, we smile and think, *That's the cutest thing in the world!* But bottle-fed milk is not meant for adults. The writer of Hebrews comes to this eloquent conclusion: you're not growing, and you're responsible!

The writer continues:

> Someone who lives on milk is still an infant and doesn't know how to do what is right.
>
> HEBREWS 5:13

We don't expect infants to enjoy solid food. After all, they have no teeth! They haven't cultivated the taste for more sophisticated foods yet. Their bodies aren't developed enough for a nuanced diet. It takes time to cultivate mature palates.

Verse 14 explains:

> Solid food is for those who are mature, who through training have the skill to recognize the difference between right and wrong.
>
> HEBREWS 5:14

This is one major reason we should grow up: this spiritual maturity enables us to discern right and wrong on our own. We learn to think clearly and correctly to determine what is good and what is bad. Such discernment isn't encouraged in a politically correct society. We are even discouraged from using words like *right* and *wrong*, because everyone's opinion is supposed to get equal time. When we are spiritually mature, however, we don't have to accept that type of inaccurate thinking. Why? Because our senses have been trained to recognize both good and evil. When I hear someone teaching the Bible, I listen carefully—not to criticize, but to discern what I'm hearing. Because of my years of training in God's Word, I am able to detect error and recognize when something is wrong. I say this not with pride but with total gratitude to God. Sometimes I notice truths that are *not* said that need to be said, and the fact that they aren't said helps me realize the weaknesses in the teaching. Such discernment is the product of the Spirit, who grows us in maturity. It's a matter of personal discipline and long-term diligence.

There's an important lesson to learn from Hebrews 5: not all spiritual nutrition is the same. Milk is the starting point for spiritual babies, but we are not to stop there; we're to grow up and mature in our faith. The result of such nutritional maturity is the ability to explain the basic truths of the Scriptures to others. Furthermore, chewing on the meat of Scripture helps us to learn right from wrong, thereby guiding our conduct. Digesting the solid food of God's Word directly affects our actions. We learn to not only know what is right but do what is right.

If you're not able to nourish your own soul, you're a spiritual baby. You still have some growing up to do. One of the deepest drives of my heart is to help other people mature in their faith. This desire inspires me to study hard every week, because I realize that biblical truth is designed to help people become more self-sustaining in their study of Scripture and more dependent on Christ. My constant prayer is this: "Guide me, Lord, as I study this passage so that I may be able to present it in a way that will help others become more aware of the value of growing up in You."

GETTING WISDOM

Recognizing the importance of feeding ourselves with spiritual food, we should next consider *what* we must eat. To help us do that, let's return to the Old Testament and examine the subject of wisdom. Proverbs is a book that drips with advice about gaining wisdom. Let's look at the very first verse in the book:

> These are the proverbs of Solomon, David's son, king of
> Israel.
>
> PROVERBS 1:1

We don't get past the first verse of Proverbs without meeting
the author: "These are the proverbs of Solomon." And who was
Solomon? He was the son of David, king of Israel—the one who
wrote most of the proverbs in this book.

What do we know about Solomon? A quick literary snapshot
appears in 1 Kings 4:29-32:

> God gave Solomon very great wisdom and understanding,
> and knowledge as vast as the sands of the seashore. In fact,
> his wisdom exceeded that of all the wise men of the East
> and the wise men of Egypt. He was wiser than anyone else,
> including Ethan the Ezrahite and the sons of Mahol—
> Heman, Calcol, and Darda. His fame spread throughout all
> the surrounding nations. He composed some 3,000 proverbs
> and wrote 1,005 songs.

What fascinating words! According to Scripture, Solomon was so
wise that people came from all around the world to glean his wisdom. After the Queen of Sheba visited Solomon, she said, "I didn't
believe what was said until I arrived here and saw it with my own
eyes. In fact, I had not heard the half of it! Your wisdom and prosperity are far beyond what I was told" (1 Kings 10:7).

This son of David was also a prolific author. As evidenced
by the thousands of proverbs and songs he wrote, he was clearly
gifted. When God led him to write the book of Proverbs, Solomon
determined to communicate the essential ingredients for life. The
single most essential ingredient is wisdom. By the way, there is no
course at any university titled Getting Wisdom. Discernment isn't

the result of completing a course. It isn't an academic pursuit, nor is it an accomplishment to check off a bucket list. Actually, some people with great knowledge have very little wisdom.

Ideally, wisdom should pass from parent to child, from grandparent to parent to grandchild to great-grandchild. Wisdom should be a family heritage that is passed down as the older generation shares their life experiences with the younger generation.

Some of the greatest wisdom I ever learned came from my father. He was the one who said to me, "Son, always be sure you have more behind the counter than you ever put on display." He wanted me to have more depth than just the words I spoke. He had the ability to put his finger on truths that only wisdom could have taught him. He passed some of those on to me.

Solomon was determined to make a difference in his son's life. Look at all the references made to "my child" or "my children" in the first three chapters of Proverbs. If we were to list all the instances that appear in the first seven chapters of Proverbs, "child" or "children" would appear no less than sixteen times. Not surprisingly, scholars call this the "my child" section of the book of Proverbs. This is a striking example of wisdom passed down from one generation to the next.

THE PASSING ON OF WISDOM IN THE BOOK OF PROVERBS

My child, listen . . . (1:8)

My child, if . . . (1:10)

My child, don't . . . (1:15)

True wisdom isn't something that comes from within us; it comes from God. Check out Proverbs 2:6: "The LORD grants wisdom!" Wisdom is sourced in God alone. Maybe your father and mother didn't relay to you the wisdom God had taught them, so how do you get it? We find the answer in a small but powerful letter in the New Testament:

> If you need wisdom, ask our generous God, and he will give it to you. He will not rebuke you for asking.
>
> JAMES 1:5

Do you have a prayer list? I'd suggest that you put this near the top: "My need for wisdom." Pray for it. Regularly request it from Him. You might offer prayers like this throughout your day: "Give me wisdom as I face this situation." "Teach me wisdom in the midst of this meeting or test." "Guide me in wisdom as I make this important decision." Frankly, I pray for wisdom almost every day.

Sometimes God delivers wisdom to us in the form of reproofs:

> Wisdom shouts in the streets.
>   She cries out in the public square.
> She calls to the crowds along the main street,
>   to those gathered in front of the city gate:
> "How long, you simpletons,
>   will you insist on being simpleminded?
> How long will you mockers relish your mocking?
>   How long will you fools hate knowledge?
> Come and listen to my counsel.
> I'll share my heart with you
>   and make you wise.

> "I called you so often, but you wouldn't come.
>   I reached out to you, but you paid no attention.
> You ignored my advice
>   and rejected the correction I offered.

So I will laugh when you are in trouble!
I will mock you when disaster overtakes you."
PROVERBS 1:20-26

Solomon personifies wisdom by giving her a voice. He says,
"Wisdom shouts in the streets," then "She cries out in the public
square." Her message to the crowds intensifies along life's main
street. She pleads, "Come and listen to my counsel."

It might seem cruel that wisdom would speak with a mocking
voice when someone is overtaken by disaster. It's not, however.
When that happens, we're actually getting what we deserve! If we're
told to listen to wisdom's counsel but we choose not to, we will
suffer serious consequences. We are free to live our lives without
wisdom. If that's our choice, we will live in the unhealthy grip
of consequences. We will endure life confused and troubled, yet
never realize why. We will be tested to the soles of our shoes and
not understand why in the world this is happening. However, if
we're sensitive to God's hand on our lives, His wisdom will rescue
us from ignorant panic. God will open our eyes to understand
that what He provides is a big dose of common sense through the
reproofs.

He grants a treasure of common sense to the honest.
He is a shield to those who walk with integrity.
PROVERBS 2:7

The benefit of walking in integrity is that you begin to glean
insights and stability from God's wisdom along the way.
Amazingly, you can become a person of wisdom, not unlike
Solomon. The result? People will seek you out. They'll ask for your
counsel. They'll listen to your explanations. They'll pay close attention even when you speak casually in conversation. Wisdom is like

a magnet, drawing others to you since they're not able to find it in their world.

So, in summary, how do we get wisdom from God? We pray for it. We find it in life's reproofs. We glean it as a by-product of integrity. Proverbs 2:1-9 spells out these ideas rather simply. Get your pen ready; you can mark these things down as you spend quiet moments in God's Word. (The difference between simply hearing and reading the Bible and *studying it* is a pen and paper.) If you've never written in your Bible before, it might seem strange to do so at first. But your Bible isn't meant to be a beautiful book that sits on your shelf; it's meant to be a tool of transformation!

First, we'll need to make some notes in the margin. Read the following passage and be ready to underscore or circle some words. This exercise will add nourishment to your spiritual diet. Read these nine verses aloud:

My son, if you will receive my words
    And treasure my commandments within you,
Make your ear attentive to wisdom,
    Incline your heart to understanding;
For if you cry for discernment,
    Lift your voice for understanding;
If you seek her as silver
    And search for her as for hidden treasures;
Then you will discern the fear of the LORD
    And discover the knowledge of God.
For the LORD gives wisdom;
    From His mouth come knowledge and understanding.
He stores up sound wisdom for the upright;
    He is a shield to those who walk in integrity,
Guarding the paths of justice,
    And He preserves the way of His godly ones.

Then you will discern righteousness and justice
   And equity and every good course.
PROVERBS 2:1-9, NASB

In this passage, Solomon offers a few specific instructions on gleaning wisdom from God. Please notice that the conditions are repeatedly described with the word *if.* Go back and mark each *if* in these verses. These instructions all represent hard work, discipline, and diligence on your part. They give clear instruction to the one seeking wisdom: if you will do these things, you will receive wisdom.

What disciplines are needed for a person to become wise? Go back and discover them for yourself. First you *receive* His words. You *treasure* His commandments. You *make your ear attentive* (stay teachable). You *incline your heart* to whatever He's ready to teach you.

Look specifically at verses 3 and 4. I've never been on a literal treasure hunt, but I have watched archaeologists hard at work, digging in the dirt and sifting through it to find valuable artifacts. I've seen these scientists work for long hours, day after day, without significant discoveries. They probe and dig and search until they suddenly come across something of value. And then what? They carefully pull it aside, treating it with great respect as they examine it. It's a time-consuming, tedious, painstaking process.

That explains why the discovery of wisdom is so rare. In our fast-paced, hurry-up world, who has the time for wisdom-digging? *Trust me—we all must make the time!* There is no substitute, no better use of our time. And the joy of discovery that awaits us is unparalleled.

Several years ago I came across the words of Robert Ballard, the man who finally discovered the great ocean liner *Titanic* on the ocean floor. He writes of his quest in these passionate words: "My first direct view of *Titanic* lasted less than two minutes, but the stark sight of her immense black hull towering above the ocean floor will remain forever engrained in my memory. My lifelong dream was to find this great ship, and during the past thirteen years the quest for her had dominated my life. Now finally, the quest was over."[2]

When Ballard finally found the ship, he took some 53,500 photos of it. Think of all of the money and the endless hours he had spent searching for it as it lay deep in the North Atlantic, off the coast of Newfoundland. Make no mistake—his discovery was the direct result of his diligent, painstaking search.

Stories like this one inspire us to stay the course—to avoid drifting along in life. Ballard's diligence and discipline set an example for us in probing deeper into the Scriptures and finding treasures to enhance our walk with God.

When I was serving my pastoral internship under Ray Stedman in Palo Alto, California, one of my assignments was to spend some time with a particular mission organization. One of the men in this group had spent more than fifty years of his life in distant countries, working with several different tribes. This man was known for his faithfulness in prayer. I remember sitting next to him, hoping that some of that diligence might rub off on me.

At one meeting, when we were studying some of the psalms together, I looked over his shoulder and peered at his open Bible. His fingers had gone over the sacred text so many times that the print had literally been rubbed off in places! That man clearly knew his Bible.

The Bible doesn't yield its treasures to the lazy soul. We can't rush through each day and assume that spiritual nourishment will happen automatically. That would be like hoping a three-course meal appears on your table but not going to the store or doing any other preparations. So what must we do to change? For starters, I recommend turning off the TV, silencing your phone, and spending at least thirty minutes a day alone and quiet, reading your Bible. Are you up for a challenge? Set aside forty-five minutes every day for one month to study God's Word, and I assure you, you will not be the same. We must search the Scriptures deliberately, consistently, and intensely. We must seek God's wisdom as we would search for precious silver or priceless artifacts.

After the first four verses in Proverbs 2, which emphasize *if*, Solomon changes his instruction from the search to the discovery. These statements are introduced by *then*.

> Then you will discern the fear of the LORD
> And discover the knowledge of God.
>
> PROVERBS 2:5, NASB

Look at that statement again. Both "the fear of the LORD" and "the knowledge of God" become our discoveries. These are the magnificent results of obtaining wisdom.

Let's examine both phrases. First, we will discern the fear of the Lord. Does *fear* mean we'll become afraid of the Lord? No. It means we will have an awesome respect for Him while at the same time developing a growing hatred for sin. Our fear of God will result in our taking Him seriously. With that will emerge an outright hatred for the things that drive us away from Him.

INSTRUCTIONS ABOUT WISDOM

How to Get Wisdom	Results of Wisdom
Proverbs 2:1-4	*Proverbs 2:5-9*
Receive (verse 1)	Discernment (verse 5)
Treasure (verse 1)	Knowledge (verse 5)
Make your ear attentive (verse 2)	Sound wisdom (verse 7)
Incline your heart (verse 2)	Protection (verse 7)
Cry (verse 3)	Discernment (verse 9)
Seek (verse 4)	
Search (verse 4)	

Second, we will discover the knowledge of God. That doesn't mean all of God's knowledge will be dumped into our brains at once. It means He will allow us to tap into His vast reservoir of knowledge and enable us to put it to use. How magnificent is that?

Look back at verse 6. God is the giver of wisdom. In verses 1-5, we are instructed to pursue wisdom, and then in verse 6, we learn that God is willing to give it. We go from being pursuers of wisdom to being receivers of wisdom. And not only wisdom, but also knowledge and understanding. What a treasure trove of valuable qualities!

WHY NOURISHMENT IS IMPORTANT

Throughout the Scriptures we find words of exhortation about discovering truth for ourselves—as well as reasons why this habit is important.

The aging fisherman-turned-apostle named Peter wrote about the importance of not only having faith but also knowing why we believe:

> Now, who will want to harm you if you are eager to do good? But even if you suffer for doing what is right, God will reward you for it. So don't worry or be afraid of their threats. Instead, you must worship Christ as Lord of your life. And if someone asks about your hope as a believer, always be ready to explain it.
>
> I PETER 3:13-15

The recipients of Peter's letter were hurting. They had been dispersed from their homes and were feeling discouraged. Peter wrote to encourage them, lest they become intimidated by and fearful of the mounting persecution. Interestingly, in the midst of his words of encouragement, Peter urged them to be ready to explain the reasons behind their fearlessness and hope. His urging wasn't just an afterthought or a casual comment meant only for those first-century Christians. This truth is applicable for all times, including today.

Let's look closely at Peter's counsel. The word *explain* comes from the Greek word *apologia*. (We get our word *apologetic* from this root word.) This isn't referring to apologizing or being sorry about something. In this case, the word *apologia* includes the idea of a formal justification, a defense. Let's add those words to this verse: "And if someone asks about your hope as a believer, always be ready to *make a formal justification* or to *give a defense*." We do this not only for our own sakes but for those around us who may not be able to defend themselves.

So why is it important to give a defense for the truth of God? Six reasons come to mind:

1. **A reasoned faith has substance.** Those who don't know the truth rely on emotions, tradition, and other people's opinions. All those sources lack substance. That becomes especially evident when we find ourselves under attack and the testing of our faith intensifies.

2. **A reasoned faith stabilizes us during times of testing.** If we know what God's Word teaches, we don't give up the faith when the bottom drops out of our lives. We are stabilized by our knowledge of the truth.

3. **A reasoned faith enables us to handle the Bible carefully and accurately.** When we know the general themes of Scripture, we are able to lean on biblical truth rather than saying what we think people want to hear.

4. **A reasoned faith equips us to detect and confront error.**
When a passage of Scripture is brought before us, we don't
need someone to interpret it for us. When we mature in our
spiritual knowledge, we can confront error with scriptural
facts.

5. **A reasoned faith makes us confident.** Knowledge of the
Scriptures keeps us secure and steady in our walk with
Christ. Such confidence grows stronger over time. The more
we learn of Him, the more confident in Him we become.

6. **A reasoned faith filters out our fears and removes long-
standing superstitions.** This is so important, since we face
the near-constant temptation to operate out of fear rather
than faith.

Another reason it's important to dig deep into God's Word is
because this practice will keep us grounded in the faith. Paul offers
a needed warning in 1 Timothy 4. This chapter was written to
Timothy, who was pastoring the church at Ephesus. The first six
verses have to do with what to expect in later times—which certainly includes our own times.

> The Holy Spirit tells us clearly that in the last times
> some will turn away from the true faith; they will follow
> deceptive spirits and teachings that come from demons.
> These people are hypocrites and liars, and their consciences
> are dead.
> They will say it is wrong to be married and wrong to
> eat certain foods. But God created those foods to be eaten
> with thanks by faithful people who know the truth. Since
> everything God created is good, we should not reject any

of it but receive it with thanks. For we know it is made acceptable by the word of God and prayer.

If you explain these things to the brothers and sisters, Timothy, you will be a worthy servant of Christ Jesus, one who is nourished by the message of faith and the good teaching you have followed.

1 TIMOTHY 4:1-6

When Scripture says that the Spirit "tells us clearly," that means this is a fact! Why else would the Word of God use this term? The passage goes on to say that "in the last times some will turn away from the true faith." The Greek term translated "turn away" is *apostatize*, meaning "to abandon, withdraw from, leave." When times get hard, some will leave the faith.

Why would anyone want to leave the one true faith? Why defect? Paul says it straight: "They will follow deceptive spirits and teachings that come from demons." The evil one is the foundational source of false information. His demons will present ideas that come from the pit, but these teachings will be communicated convincingly as truth. How? The answer comes in verse 2: by means of hypocrites and liars whose consciences have been seared as with a branding iron. They have no qualms about leading others into the realm of error, and they convince gullible hearers with their charisma and charm.

The Spirit explicitly warns us of such people in verse 3: "They will say it is wrong to be married and wrong to eat certain foods." In spite of such opposition in the last days, we don't find the apostle Paul biting his nails and feeling anxious, wondering, *How am I going to make it through all this?* Rather, he calmly refutes these deceivers. Verse 3 says, "But God created those foods to be eaten with thanks by faithful people who know the truth." The truth is, God has created marriage, and God has given us foods to eat. We have been delivered from a law that kept us from eating certain foods. So we don't have a thing to be afraid of. That's the reason Paul is so calm: he has a firm grip on scriptural doctrine. He knows where he stands. His soul has been nourished by God's wisdom. With calm confidence, he writes, "Since everything God created is good, we should not reject any of it but receive it with thanks. For we know it is made acceptable by the word of God and prayer."

How calm can we be in the midst of such distressing times? Paul was calm because he knew where he stood. In fact, Paul offers help to all ministers of the gospel through his words to Timothy: "If you explain these things to the brothers and sisters, Timothy, you will be a worthy servant of Christ Jesus." He goes on to instruct Timothy that he needs to be "nourished by the message of faith and the good teaching you have followed."

Isn't that good advice? In a sense, these words are a divine job description for every true minister of the gospel. We are to constantly nourish ourselves in God's Book. The longer we do God's work, the more need we have to be nourished. The greater the pressure, the more the problems, the more the calendar gets filled with other things, the more we must devour this Book so our minds stay sharp with the truth and so we can deliver it—personally as well as publicly. Most important, only then will we be able to live it out.

I close this chapter with a few personal comments. I could not be more thankful for the seminary where I studied, for mentors who loved the truth and helped me cultivate it, for parents who taught me the way, for a wife who helped put me through my seminary education, and for congregations who were patient as I forged out my theology, right up to this present moment. I am grateful for so many people who had a hand in my learning and growing process.

Where are you in this growth process? Are you taking in sufficient nourishment? Do you know your way around the kitchen enough to make spiritual meals for yourself? Are you helping others prepare their meals as well? I hope so!

I love the way C. S. Lewis puts it: "If all the world were Christian, it might not matter if all the world were uneducated. But, as it is, a cultural life will exist outside the Church whether it exists inside or not. To be ignorant and simple now—not to be able to meet the enemies on their own ground—would be to throw down our weapons, and to betray our uneducated brethren who have, under God, no defence but us against the intellectual attacks of the heathen." He adds, "Good philosophy must exist, if for no other reason, because bad philosophy needs to be answered. The cool intellect must work not only against cool intellect on the other side, but against the muddy heathen mysticisms which deny intellect altogether. Most of all, perhaps, we need intimate knowledge of the past."[3]

The Bible is filled with an enormous amount of healthy nutrition. To tap into it will require us to change our diets and spend sufficient time in preparation. I urge you to take on a new role as your own chef—one who specializes in nutritious meals. Get in the kitchen and start cooking today! The next chapter will help you know how to get started.

Before we begin preparing a good, healthy meal, we need to think through what will be served and how nourishing it will be. Here are five exercises for you to try as you learn about the nutritional value of investing time in God's Word for yourself.

1. Read Proverbs 1–2 in your Bible. Create a table with two headings: "What am I supposed to do?" and "What will the result be?" As you carefully read the passage, write down each action you're instructed to do in the first column. Then write down the result of each action in the second column. Here's an example for each column:

PRACTICAL WISDOM	
What am I supposed to do?	*What will the result be?*
Get insight (Proverbs 1:4)	Live in peace (Proverbs 1:33)

_____
_____
_____
_____
_____

What do these first two chapters of Proverbs teach?

2. Read Hosea 4:1-4. Make a list of all the things the people of Israel did that displeased the Lord.

Next read Amos 8:11-13.

What happens in the case of a famine when people don't hear the words of the Lord?

According to these two minor prophets, what can we learn about the importance of digging deeply into God's Word?

3. Sometimes people in the Bible can help us understand the message God is giving us. Having considered the value of wisdom, we're able to learn much more by examining the life of Solomon, the wisest man who ever lived. Read 1 Kings 3–4 carefully—and aloud—to find out about his character.

Write a brief paragraph describing Solomon. Include the role wisdom played in his life as described in this passage. Then write down three things we can learn about wisdom from Solomon.

4. The Word of God has a profound effect on individuals but also on nations. Read the story of King Josiah finding the Book of the Law (a phrase that refers to the Scriptures) in 2 Kings 22:1-20.

Write down five results of the people in Josiah's day finding and hearing God's Word. What does this teach us about the Scriptures?

5. Another way to learn about the importance of God's Word is to see what happens when people misuse it. Peter writes of the harm caused by false teachers in 2 Peter 2:1-22. Read this passage and then go back through the verses again very thoughtfully.

Make a list of the negative fallout Peter mentions from false teachers (he names no less than ten).

6. Jesus preaches the greatest sermon ever preached with the Sermon on the Mount (recorded in Matthew 5–7). At the end of the sermon, Jesus reminds His listeners that God's Word requires a response. Read the parable Jesus tells about wisdom (Matthew 7:24-25) and then picture it in your mind.

According to what Jesus taught, what is the result of wisdom?

STAGE TWO

Preparing the Meal

CHAPTER 3

CHOOSING THE RECIPE

Pursuing the Treasures of Scripture

ANY CHEF WILL TELL YOU that there is a right way and a wrong way to prepare a meal. While there is always room for creative style and flavor preferences, there are definite procedures used to combine all the ingredients into something delicious. The recipe is the key. Good recipes are essential for consistently turning out good meals.

We need to follow the same guidelines when studying the Scriptures. Our recipe will be based on the process that has shaped my personal study of God's Word as well as my fifty-plus years of teaching the Bible to others. Truth be told, a week never passes without my using one or more of the principles that I'm going to pass along to you. None of my messages are prepared without my first going through this process. When I saw how transforming this teaching could be for people, I realized that I have no right to keep it from those who desire to get into the Word of God on their own.

This chapter provides a general recipe for pursuing the treasures of Scripture. Each of the next four chapters will explain the four-part method in detail, with several examples so you can put the steps into practice for yourself. The following four chapters build on one another, so it's important to follow the steps in order. There's nothing worse than skipping an important step in a recipe only to have dinner turn out to be a flop.

OUR RECIPE

The first step of our Bible study method is to observe the text of Scripture. We will then probe the meaning of the Scripture to help us interpret what we have observed. Then we'll learn the value of comparing or correlating the truths of Scripture. And finally we'll discover how to apply the wisdom of Scripture.

Four words describe this process: *observation, interpretation, correlation*, and *application*. I suggest that you memorize these steps. The Bible wasn't given simply to satisfy idle curiosity. The Bible wasn't written so clergy would have something to say on Sundays. The Bible has been preserved to transform the lives of people like you and me. Never forget that!

OUR BIBLE STUDY METHOD

1. Observation
2. Interpretation
3. Correlation
4. Application

In casual readings of the Bible, it's easy to miss many of its treasured nuggets. As a result, in most homes, the Bible is nothing more than a thick book that sits on a shelf or table, collecting dust. That's why one wag has called it "the world's best-selling coffee table book." But it was never meant to be used as decoration. It was never meant to prompt others to say, "Whoa, look at that Bible!" It was given to us to be put to use. A Bible that's doing its job becomes well worn and well marked. Its pages begin to fray, just like a favorite family cookbook. The more we study God's Word, the better acquainted with it we become. And once we've learned how to dig into it ourselves, we will be able to teach others how to do the same.

A SHORT STUDY OF A LONG PSALM

It's helpful to remember that the Bible itself states the importance of learning and teaching the Scriptures. Let's begin our search of this biblical theme by looking at Psalm 119. As we work our way through this psalm, we quickly discover that it's a long chapter. In fact, it's the longest of all the psalms—176 verses.

This psalm fits into what the Israelites called their *psalter*, which is an ancient word for "hymnal." It was from this book, the Psalms, that the Israelites sang their songs and learned their hymns. In fact, the word *psalms* simply means "songs." Every song that's of some length has stanzas, and every stanza has several verses.

Psalm 119 may seem a little strange at first glance. At the very beginning it features an unfamiliar word, *Aleph*. Eight verses later, in verse 9, we come to the word *Beth*. This is followed by *Gimel* in verse 17. What are these titles? They represent the first three of the twenty-two characters in the Hebrew alphabet. Psalm 119 is a beautiful acrostic poem containing twenty-two stanzas, each beginning with the next letter in the Hebrew alphabet. Every stanza has eight verses, all of which begin with the same Hebrew letter. Eight verses per stanza times twenty-two stanzas brings us to 176 verses.

Why would the psalmist have gone to the trouble of writing a carefully worded acrostic like this one? The ancient Hebrews loved the Lord and took the Scriptures very seriously. Because few people had the ability to read the scrolls, they would primarily hear God's Word read and would commit large sections of the Scriptures to memory. Acrostics like this were aids in Scripture memory for children as they grew up. When children were in school, learning their alphabet, they would be able to review each letter of the alphabet by working their way through Psalm 119. Centuries ago in Germany, this psalm was referred to as "the Christian's golden ABC of praise, love, power,

| PSALM 119 AS AN ACROSTIC POEM ||
Hebrew Alphabet	Psalm 119
א – Aleph	Verses 1-8
ב – Beth	Verses 9-16
ג – Gimel	Verses 17-24
ד – Daleth	Verses 25-32
ה – He	Verses 33-40
ו – Waw	Verses 41-48
ז – Zayin	Verses 49-56
ח – Heth	Verses 57-64
ט – Teth	Verses 65-72
י – Yodh	Verses 73-80
כ – Kaph	Verses 81-88
ל – Lamedh	Verses 89-96
מ – Mem	Verses 97-104
נ – Nun	Verses 105-112
ס – Samekh	Verses 113-120
ע – Ayin	Verses 121-128
פ – Pe	Verses 129-136
צ – Tsadhe	Verses 137-144
ק – Qoph	Verses 145-152
ר – Resh	Verses 153-160
ש – Shin	Verses 161-168
ת – Taw	Verses 169-176

and use of the Word of God."[4] Think of this psalm as an ABC of the love of God, the power of God, the praise of God, and the importance of His Word in everyday life.

Another interesting fact about Psalm 119 is that all but four of the verses are directed to the Lord Himself. With the exception of verses 1 through 3 and verse 115, all the rest are written to and about Him. Let's look at the first three verses:

Joyful are people of integrity,
    who follow the instructions of the LORD.
Joyful are those who obey his laws
    and search for him with all their hearts.
They do not compromise with evil,
    and they walk only in his paths.

PSALM 119:1-3

These verses make a statement regarding those who take God seriously. When we get to verse 4, we come across a telltale clue that this psalm is a prayer. This psalm is directed to the Lord, beginning with the word *you.*

You have charged us
    to keep your commandments carefully.
Oh, that my actions would consistently
    reflect your decrees!
Then I will not be ashamed
    when I compare my life with your commands.
As I learn your righteous regulations,
    I will thank you by living as I should!

PSALM 119:4-7

We address the Lord in a similar way every time we pray. We begin with words like "Dear God" or "Dear heavenly Father, we thank You" or "We praise You, Father, because of Your grace" or "Today, we bring before You our need." This is an excellent psalm to use as a guide for prayer.

Another major theme in this psalm is the Word of God. There is hardly a verse in this chapter that doesn't reference God's Word through one of several synonyms. Look at verse 1 again: "The instructions of the LORD" is a synonym for the Word of God.

Verse 2 says, "his laws"—another synonym for the Scriptures. "Your commandments" in verse 4 and "your commands" are clearly references to God's Word. I love what God's Word is called in verse 7: "righteous regulations."

As we continue our reading, we observe how deliberate the psalmist is in exalting God's Word:

How can a young person stay pure?
By obeying your word.
I have tried hard to find you—
don't let me wander from your commands.
I have hidden your word in my heart,
that I might not sin against you.
I praise you, O LORD;
teach me your decrees.
I have recited aloud
all the regulations you have given us.
I have rejoiced in your laws
as much as in riches.
I will study your commandments
and reflect on your ways.
I will delight in your decrees
and not forget your word.

PSALM 119:9-16

While verse 9 highlights obedience to the Scriptures, verse 11 shows the importance of knowing and memorizing God's Word. In verse 12, we read about "your decrees," and verse 13 refers to "the regulations." Verses 14-15 describe "your laws" and "your commandments." All the way through these 176 verses, we discover various words related to the Word of God. The psalmist is caught up in praise to God for giving His people His Word.

Let me add here that making such observations will take time. Remember what I've been emphasizing: discipline and diligence are required when we prepare our own meals from the Bible, just as time and effort are required when we cook physical meals. That's why the fast-food industry is on the rise. Our older daughter tells us, with tongue in cheek, that when her kids were little, she'd say, "Okay, kids, supper's ready," and upon hearing this, they'd all hop in the car to go to a restaurant. That's the quick and easy way. To prepare a meal ourselves is a completely different story.

Think about it. First, you have to make a grocery list. That means you must first consider what the menu will be. You have to think about what's nutritious as well as what you can afford, not to mention ensuring that you have a nice variety of foods in your diet. After finding and purchasing everything, you come home facing the work of preparation. You need to peel, clean, chop, cook, bake, broil, or fry whatever you have decided to eat. (Here in Texas, we fry most of our meals!) If you don't learn these steps, you'll be eating someone else's cooking.

That's the same reason some people remain biblically illiterate. Those who don't learn to prepare their own meals from the Scriptures simply don't know what God's Word has to say. Our souls crave more food than just the nourishment we get in an hour on a Sunday morning.

What's the big deal about preparing your own meals? Stop and imagine. What if someday you aren't allowed to have a Bible? What if someday you're living behind bars because the government has been overthrown and the new leaders have made it illegal to possess a Bible? In that extreme situation, how will you survive on spiritual food? From your own previous study, from your own learning and memorizing of the Scriptures. And I will tell you that if you are studying right now, you will be an invaluable presence in that cell. You will be one of the few who knows the Scriptures.

It's amazing what happens when any serious pain enters the heart. One wise soul has written, "[Pain] plants the flag of truth in the fortress of a rebel soul."[5] It's amazing how soft our hearts can become when we're in great need. Spiritual truth sustains us in dire circumstances.

My desire is to equip you with what you need to prepare and then cook your own meals. If we happen to meet each other sometime in the future and you say, "Let me tell you about the meal I just prepared on my own," no one will be more excited for you than I! As you do the work of Bible study for yourself, you will be growing up . . . becoming a spiritual adult.

CONDITIONS OF THE HEART

I have just a few more suggestions before you get started. First of all, in order for you to do your own work in the Scriptures, it's essential to consider some conditions of the heart.

1. **The first prerequisite is personal integrity.** Look back at the first verse of our psalm: "Joyful are people of integrity, who follow the instructions of the LORD." There is an old but true axiom I often repeat to myself: "Sin will keep you from the Word of God, or the Word of God will keep you from sin." To glean truth from the Book of Truth, we need to have pure hearts. In order to understand the Scriptures, we must know the Lord and be walking the path of daily purity. Integrity and purity go hand in hand.

2. **You also need willingness—a personal desire to follow the Lord.** See what the psalmist says in the second verse? "Joyful are those who obey his laws and search for him with all their hearts." I can tell you from experience over these many years that when I open the Scriptures, I can't wait to get into them.

Why? Because I have cultivated a willingness to allow the Word of God to get into me! I love to be around people with that same willingness. When we become motivated to study God's Word, such excitement is contagious and begins to rub off on others.

3. **The third essential for studying the Scriptures is passion.** You must have the passion to search for nuggets of truth. The end of verse 2 states that those who obey God's Word "search for him with all their hearts." This is not a casual search! We are to go after truth the way someone in love pursues his or her beloved.

4. **Another condition needed is time.** You will need time to pray, meditate, and turn thoughts over in your mind. Verse 11 states, "I have hidden your word in my heart," and verse 12 asks the Lord to "teach me your decrees." These aren't things that happen overnight; we need to invest time to make them happen.

So the essential conditions of the heart include (1) living in purity, (2) being willing to follow the Lord, (3) being passionate about pursuing the truth, and (4) investing time in His Word.

HELPFUL TOOLS FOR STUDY

Having met those conditions of the heart, we'll need some tools. Just as a cook needs the right pots and pans, we will be more effective in our Bible study if we have the appropriate equipment.

1. **You need a Bible.** Specifically, you need a Bible that is in a translation you can understand. I highly recommend a study Bible with notes at the bottom of each page. The Bible I use for study has notes in it, while the one I preach from does not. Make sure you use a Bible that has a print size you can

easily read. It's helpful if it has some room in the margin so you can make your own notes. It's also important to have *your own* Bible. Although Cynthia and I may refer to each other's Bibles when we're looking for a verse together, we use separate Bibles when we're studying so we can write personal notes and observations.

2. **You need a dictionary.** Every home should have a dictionary. Let me add to this: you also need a *Bible* dictionary. The one I use is *Unger's Bible Dictionary.* I studied under the author, Merrill F. Unger, when I learned Hebrew at Dallas Seminary. You may choose another Bible dictionary or even an online Bible dictionary (you may want to try http://www.biblestudytools.com /dictionaries or http://www.biblestudytools.com/dictionaries /bakers-evangelical-dictionary). Just be sure you find one that's easy for you to read. This resource will identify places and names in the Bible and explain words that may be unfamiliar in our modern-day context. Words are important—they form the building blocks of spiritual thoughts. The meaning of a word has everything to do with the meaning of the sentence. And the meaning of the sentence has everything to do with the paragraph in which it is placed. Keep a dictionary handy to ensure that the deeper spiritual truths aren't lost on you.

BIBLE DICTIONARY SAMPLE ENTRY

Servant

In the Bible, servants were usually slaves, meaning they were the property of other people. Both the Old Testament and the New Testament address the protection and fair treatment of slaves as well as admonish slaves to obey their masters. In the Old Testament, Jesus is prophesied as the *Servant* of the Lord. This title anticipated Christ's perfect belonging and obedience to the Father.

3. **You need a concordance.** A concordance is an alphabetical listing of all the words in the Bible. If you want to find the word
integrity in the Scriptures, you can look it up in a concordance.
Under the letter *i* you'll find *integrity*, and you'll see a list of
every time it appears in the Bible. That may not seem all that
important to you now, but as you get into serious Bible study,
a concordance will be an invaluable resource. You will want to
know what the Bible says on whatever topic or subject you're
studying. Note that you'll want a concordance that matches
the Bible version you use to ensure that the words correspond
exactly.

CONCORDANCE SAMPLE ENTRY

Integrity

Deuteronomy 9:5
2 Samuel 22:26
1 Kings 9:4
2 Chronicles 19:7
Psalm 119:1
Proverbs 2:7, 21
Proverbs 10:9, 29
1 Timothy 3:8

---

4. **Finally, you need a good set of maps.** Look in the back of
your Bible, and you may find several maps there. If you
don't have maps in your Bible, I strongly suggest that you
look for one with this feature or access one online. A good
study Bible usually has ten to fifteen maps in the back.
It is helpful to have a current map of the land of Israel so
you can understand where the corresponding locations
are today. Here are some of the other maps that will be

ISRAEL AND THE MIDDLE EAST TODAY

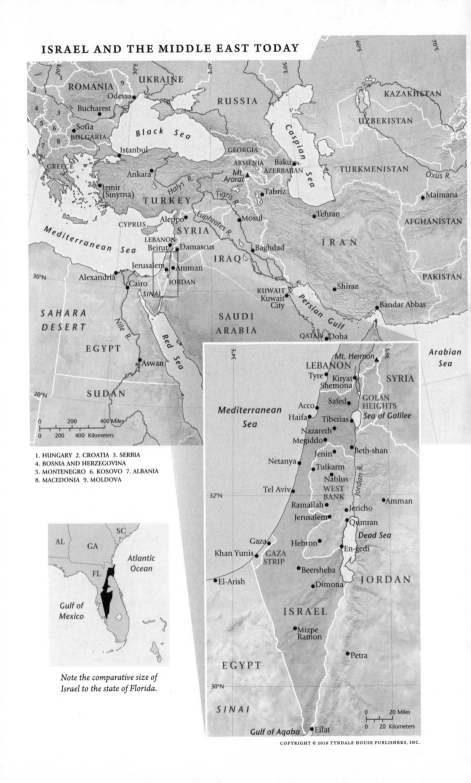

1. HUNGARY 2. CROATIA 3. SERBIA
4. BOSNIA AND HERZEGOVINA
5. MONTENEGRO 6. KOSOVO 7. ALBANIA
8. MACEDONIA 9. MOLDOVA

Note the comparative size of
Israel to the state of Florida.

beneficial for you as you study: a map of the territories occupied by the ancient patriarchs, a map of the Exodus out of Egypt, a map covering the life of Jesus, and a map of Paul's journeys. In your study, you will often find that you need to familiarize yourself with the geography of a story so you can understand more of the context. Since some places mentioned in Scripture have similar names, a map will help you find the locations, and a Bible dictionary will explain how the places differ.

In order to be successful with your own cooking, you will need the right utensils. Perhaps I should also mention that just as a cook needs a place to create meals, you need a place to study. You may not have a large place—that's no problem. You may not have a lot of quiet. But you do need a place where you can get away from distractions and study. I know a man who does his study in his car because that's the only quiet place he can find.

During my growing-up years, my mother did most of her study in our one bathroom. We often knocked on the door, saying, "Mom, are you finished?" She would come out with her Bible under one arm and a dictionary under another. I'd say, "Mom, please!" And she'd reply, "There's no other place as quiet where I can be alone, and I also have my own seat in there!"

Wherever you choose to study, keep your study tools close by. You can keep your Bible, your dictionary, your Bible dictionary, your concordance, and your maps or Bible atlas nearby so everything you need to dig into God's Word will be at your fingertips.

GOD'S PERSONAL PROMISES

One of the immediate joys we will find as we dig into the Scriptures is that God is speaking directly to us. There are promises in the Bible—personal promises we can claim as a result of learning the Scriptures. This is one of the most exciting parts of doing our own study. God has promised us certain benefits that are ours as a result of getting to know His Word. As you pore over the Scriptures and take them seriously, He will bless you in special ways. By studying His Book, you are equipping yourself for life.

Here is a personal promise we're invited to claim:

Oh, that my actions would consistently
    reflect your decrees!
Then I will not be ashamed
    when I compare my life with your commands.
PSALM 119:5-6

Notice the word *decrees* in this passage—another synonym for God's Word. Did you catch this great promise? When we live according to the Bible, we will be freed from shame. Some people live their lives in a cave of shame. There are few enemies of the soul worse than shame, as it keeps us trapped in guilt and hopelessness. But the better we get to know the Word of God, the more freedom we will experience. God will deliver us from the dreadful, galling shackles of shame. What a promise!

Let's look further into this magnificent psalm:

Oh, how I love your instructions!
    I think about them all day long.
Your commands make me wiser than my
        enemies,
    for they are my constant guide.
Yes, I have more insight than my teachers,
    for I am always thinking of your laws.

I am even wiser than my elders,
    for I have kept your commandments.
I have refused to walk on any evil path,
    so that I may remain obedient to your word.
I haven't turned away from your regulations,
    for you have taught me well.
How sweet your words taste to me;
    they are sweeter than honey.
Your commandments give me understanding;
    no wonder I hate every false way of life.

Your word is a lamp to guide my feet
    and a light for my path.

PSALM 119:97-105

The psalmist states three amazing promises in a row. The first promise is in verse 98: "Your commands make me wiser than my enemies." The promise here is that we will have wisdom beyond those who stalk us—those who say ugly words against us. By taking God's Word seriously, we will gain wisdom over our enemies, which will enable us to live above the intimidation and the threat of their presence in our lives. What a promise!

Read verse 99 for the second promise: "I have more insight than my teachers." Not only will we have wisdom that's greater than our enemies, but we'll have insight greater than our teachers. This isn't necessarily about intellect or knowledge; it's about God giving us the filter of Scripture to recognize whether things are true. You'll have more insight than your professors or supervisors, and you won't be bullied by anyone whose goal is to shipwreck your faith. You'll be able to stand your ground. God promises to give us insight for life!

The next verse gives the third promise: "I am even wiser than my elders." That means just what it says. You don't have to wait until you're in your sixties, seventies, or eighties to gain sufficient wisdom; you can gain it before you grow old. If you become a student of the Scriptures in your thirties, you'll be a leg up on people decades older than you when it comes to understanding. Here's a pearl of wisdom from the book of Job:

> Sometimes the elders are not wise.
>   Sometimes the aged do not understand justice.
>
> JOB 32:9

When you get into the Scriptures on your own, you will begin to glean judgment. You'll get wisdom as well as insight and understanding. Let me tell you the difference between these three attributes. We tend to use these words interchangeably, but they're not really interchangeable. Wisdom is the ability to look at life as God looks at life. Insight is the ability to see through life's circumstances—to look beyond the obvious or the apparent. Understanding is the crowning blessing—the ability to respond to life correctly. As we gain wisdom and insight, the understanding that comes will enable us to handle life in a God-honoring way. That's why Proverbs says that we need to "get wisdom" but that in all our wisdom, we need to "develop good judgment" (Proverbs 4:5). As we begin to make a study of God's Word and learn from it, it will equip us with these magnificent benefits.

THE BENEFITS OF STUDYING GOD'S WORD

Wisdom: the ability to look at life the way God looks at life
Insight: the ability to see through life's circumstances
Understanding: the ability to respond to life correctly

LEARNING TO CHEW AND SWALLOW THE SCRIPTURES

Once we have learned to fix our own meals and have sat down to eat, we savor God's truths. There are at least five ways to get God's Word into our systems.

1. **Hearing.** We begin to consume the Scriptures by hearing them. Hearing what God's Word says is the simplest, most common way to learn the Bible. It's also the least interactive method of grasping the truth. Look at verse 24: "Your laws please me; they give me wise advice" (Psalm 119:24). As you commit yourself to the teaching of God's Word, you are learning what will be for you a pleasant future. Psalm 119:130 says, "The teaching of your word gives light, so even the simple can understand." The apostle Paul affirms this idea in his letter to the Romans: "Faith comes by hearing, and hearing by the word of God" (Romans 10:17, NKJV). We begin to grasp the Scriptures as we hear God's written message.

2. **Reading.** Second, we read it. The Bible is not a conglomeration of mysterious and convoluted words strung together; it's a book filled with sentences you can read. And from those sentences and paragraphs you can learn how to live differently than you've lived before. You can learn how to handle those who are difficult to be around. You can learn how to endure a divorce without being eaten up with bitterness or scarred by what led to that painful decision. You can be guided and strengthened through suffering. You can be stabilized when you get the report from the MRI. The Bible will strengthen you because you have been hearing it and reading it for yourself. Consider Psalm 119:18: "Open my eyes to see the wonderful truths in your instructions." Never underestimate

the wonders that will come to you as a result of reading the Scriptures.

3. **Studying.** Another way to consume Scripture is by studying it. There's a difference between hearing, reading, and studying. This last method involves the use of your fingers and the engagement of your brain. I learned years ago, as Dawson Trotman (founder of the Navigators) said, "Thoughts disentangle themselves when they pass through the lips and the fingertips." My tangled thoughts regarding struggles, loss, disappointment, discouragement, and life in general can be unscrambled if I dialogue about them. They become even clearer if I talk with someone who will really enter into that discussion with me or if I write them out in my journal.

Many years ago, I found these words by Sir Francis Bacon: "Reading maketh a full man; conference a ready man; and writing an exact man." When you begin to process through writing, it helps to clarify your thoughts. You may jot down questions that come to you as you're reading. You may write down observations or note a reference to another section of Scripture you want to consider. As you study, you encounter questions about background, context, and geography that aren't easily answered. Your reading may also spark connections to your own life. Jot down these notes as you work your way through the Scriptures so you can dig into them more deeply later. True study involves a pen and a pad.

4. **Memorizing.** You truly begin to consume Scripture by memorizing verses of the Bible. Don't think you can? Well, do you know your home address? Do you know your e-mail address? How about your phone number?

Have you memorized the way to work? Of course! So stop telling yourself you can't memorize. We memorize whatever we believe is worth the effort. When the psalmist says, "I have recited aloud all the regulations you have given us" (119:13), he's saying, "I've been committing to memory verses from the scrolls."

When you begin to treasure God's Word in your heart, you will find that light penetrates the darkness of your surroundings. You will be given a shield against the dangers around you as a result of the memorized Word. God's Word sealed on your lips will rescue you from despair. Memorizing Scripture will turn discouragement into encouragement. As you hear, read, and study God's Word, there are certain verses you'll want to memorize. I've known people who had hundreds of verses of Scripture memorized. Without exception, when I ask, "How did you do that?" they answer, "One verse at a time." First you read the verse repeatedly. You may choose to write it on a card and then take that card with you. You can put it next to your computer screen or on the visor of your car. You can post it on the refrigerator in your kitchen or by the sink so you can memorize while you do dishes.

My mother was a master at memorizing Scripture, and she offered challenges to me when I was growing up. If there was one thing I needed back then, it was a challenge. She said, "I'll tell you what, Son. For every verse you learn, I'll learn two." And I thought, "Okay, Mom . . . I'm going to memorize you under the table." I'd memorize six verses, and she'd surprise me by memorizing twelve. I'd memorize a chapter, and she'd memorize two chapters. I'd memorize several chapters, and she'd memorize a whole book of the Bible. Today I am so grateful that she challenged me to memorize Scripture. Every verse I've memorized, I've used. Every verse I haven't memorized and then needed later, I've regretted. So let me charge you now as my mother charged me: you will always be grateful for the sections of God's Word that are hidden in your heart.

5. **Meditating.** The final way we will come to take in Scripture is to meditate on it. Psalm 119:15 states, "I will study your commandments and reflect on your ways." That's meditation: taking time to reflect on God's Word and let it soak into our hearts. Verse 23 confirms the psalmist's commitment to saturating himself with God's Word: "Even princes sit and speak against me, but I will meditate on your decrees" (Psalm 119:23).

I don't need to worry about what people say against me. Why would I worry about those things? They're in God's hands. How do I know? Because I've chewed on God's Word. I've blended it with the mind that God has given me. Meditation helps us go to sleep at night, and it's a wonderful way to wake up in the morning.

WAYS TO TAKE IN GOD'S WORD

---

1. Hear God's Word.
2. Read the Bible.
3. Study the Scriptures.
4. Memorize verses.
5. Meditate daily.

THE BASICS OF OUR RECIPE

Let's go over the foundational recipe we need to follow as we get serious about preparing our own meals. There are four key steps:

1. **Observation.** Observation answers the question "What does the Bible say?" It's the process of seeing what the Bible actually says. You're not answering questions at this point. You're not adding something through your imagination. You're simply reading the words on the page. Observation is carefully reading and thinking about what the Bible actually says. We'll cover this in detail in the next chapter.

2. **Interpretation.** Interpretation is learning what the Bible means. Each verse of Scripture means something, and when one verse is tied together with other verses, there's an even deeper meaning. In this book you'll learn some techniques of interpretation. You won't have to rely on my interpretations—you can do it yourself. We will examine this process in chapter 5.

3. **Correlation.** Correlation is comparing one verse of Scripture with another. This is one of the reasons you'll need a concordance. When we see that Psalm 119 and 2 Timothy 3 are making similar statements about God's Word, the meaning becomes clearer to you than ever. And the words in 2 Timothy 3 cause Joshua 1:8 to come to life as these verses are synthesized together. We'll learn how to do this in chapter 6.

4. **Application.** I call application the crowning benefit of Bible study. While correlation is realizing what the Bible says elsewhere about a topic, application is putting the Bible to use in everyday life—in your decisions, your struggles, your finances, your relationships, your home and family, your gains, your losses, your leadership, your forgiveness. All of those areas—and a thousand others. We'll address this process in chapter 7.

It's easy to take it for granted that we have access to the Bible. But in various times in history—and in some countries today—people have given their lives to preserve God's Word. Even in England, there was a time when the Bible was to be chained to a pulpit and handled only by the clergy. The Scriptures were in Latin, and it was against the law for the Bible to be in the language of the common people.

In the midst of this repression of God's Word, a hero named William Tyndale came along. He was an early English Reformer who lived from 1494 to 1536. He was troubled by the vast ignorance of the Scriptures among the people around him, and he knew it would be impossible to change that unless the Scriptures were "plainly laid before their eyes in their mother tongue."[6] The printing of his first English New Testament came off the press in 1525, even though it was against the law. A police raid stopped his work, so Tyndale had to resume his Bible translation in secret. He finished the following year and then began to write commentaries on Old and New Testament books.

Tyndale's output was impressive, especially considering the setbacks he faced—a shipwreck, the loss of manuscripts, being chased by secret agents, having his printer raided by the police, and being betrayed by friends. Despite these challenges, he was determined to get God's Word into the language of the people. His translation was lucid, crisp, and concise, and above all, it appealed to ordinary, down-to-earth people. His literary work, however, was never respected or recognized by the elite of his day.

In 1535, Tyndale was arrested near the city of Brussels and imprisoned. The following year he was strangled to death, and his body was burned to ashes. The thinking of the religious elite was, "Let's get rid of Tyndale, and we'll get rid of this English Bible." On the contrary, he who is dead still speaks. The English Bible exists because William Tyndale gave his life for it. How he treasured God's truth! The least we can do is learn it.

Our learning begins with the discipline of following a recipe. The four-step process will help prevent error in our understanding. With proper preparation and careful application, we will come to savor the Scriptures. Are you ready to take the first step?

Since we've been comparing our study of the Bible to preparing a meal, now it's time for you to step into the kitchen and get cooking! Here are six exercises to help you apply what you just read. I encourage you to give each one your best effort.

1. Take time to carefully read Psalm 119:1-40. Make a list of everything this psalm says about God's Word. (Remember that God's Word can also be referred to as commandments, laws, instructions, decrees, and regulations.) For example, "People who obey God's Word are joyful" (verse 1); "God has charged us to obey His commandments" (verse 4).

2. What kind of wisdom can a person get from studying God's Word? Use Psalm 119:97-105 as your guide.

3. On page 59, there is a sample concordance entry for the

word *integrity*. Look up each of the following references and note God's calling for believers in each one:

> Deuteronomy 9:5
> 2 Samuel 22:26
> 1 Kings 9:4
> 2 Chronicles 19:7
> Psalm 119:1
> Proverbs 2:7, 21
> Proverbs 10:9, 29
> 1 Timothy 3:8

What do these verses teach you about the biblical call to a life of integrity?

4. As we learned in this chapter, it's helpful to look up words in the dictionary, and especially in a Bible dictionary, to learn their meanings. Note the key word *sacrifice* in the following verse:

This is real love—not that we loved God, but that he loved us and sent his Son as a *sacrifice* to take away our sins.
1 JOHN 4:10 (emphasis added)

Turn to this verse in your own Bible and notice the word that is used. Some translations use "atonement," while others say "propitiation." Look up the word used in your Bible in a Bible dictionary. How is it defined?

Once you understand the meaning of this important word that describes what Jesus accomplished on the cross, find out how the same word is used in Romans 3:25, Hebrews 2:17, and 1 John 2:2. Describe sacrifice (or whatever word is used in your Bible) in your own words, using these passages to assist you.

5. A map can help you understand the context for the stories and events that take place in the Scriptures. Turn to the maps in the back of your Bible or to online maps. Locate one that traces the second journey of Paul. Follow that long journey with your finger, and as you do, take note of the places he traveled. You'll see that when he arrived at Troas in the western part of Asia Minor (the country known as Turkey today), he had to sail across the Aegean Sea to reach Europe. Once there, he went to Philippi and then on to Greece, where he continued to preach the gospel. Again, trace the remainder of his lengthy second journey with your finger. Pause and imagine how rugged his journey must have been in the first century as he traveled that distance.

6. Read and study Psalm 19:7-11. What promises are given to the believer who studies God's Word? List at least five descriptions of God's Word from these verses.

Additional tip: Make an inventory of the resources that are available to you, using the list provided in this chapter. What features does your Bible include (maps, index, concordance, etc.) that will be helpful for your personal study? Where can you go to find further information about the Bible (concordance, dictionary, online resources)? Gather your resources together and create a physical space for study with limited distractions. Make this the place where you can daily feast on the Word of God.

CHAPTER 4

READING THE INGREDIENTS

Observing the Text

HAVE YOU EVER MARVELED at how someone can see something in a passage of Scripture that you've read many times but never noticed yourself? It's like the person reached up to the top shelf of the pantry cabinet and pulled down something you've glanced past many times but failed to see for yourself. Sometimes that can be discouraging; other times it simply makes you curious. If only you could pull out the same ingredient, you could make your own gourmet meal. Just as a knowledge of the ingredients is a prerequisite for making a delicious meal, a careful reading of the Scriptures is required for proper understanding. My hope is that this chapter will help you take the first step toward reaching *top-shelf* understanding on your own. It really isn't complicated; it just takes some intentionality.

While I realize that most people aren't called to preach or stand before a group of people and teach God's Word, all of us in God's family are to be good students of His Word. The first step in getting to know your Bible is *observation*, which we discussed in the previous chapter. Through observation, we discover what the Bible says. This part of the process is absolutely foundational. I go through this process every time I prepare any message, lesson, or sermon. Yes . . . *every* time. One hundred percent of the time, I start right there. My goal is to discover what is written in the verses I'm studying.

Many people are in such a hurry to know the meaning of the Bible that they rush ahead and overlook the step of observation as they plunge straight into interpretation. That's a guaranteed formula for error. It's the equivalent of randomly mixing ingredients together before you're sure you have the right ones in the right amounts. You can never reach the correct interpretation of the Scriptures until you've taken sufficient time to discover what the Bible is saying. Learning what has been written must always precede finding out what it means. Interpretation hinges on thorough, careful observation.

SHARPENING YOUR OBSERVATION SKILLS

What do I mean when I refer to observation? To observe means "to inspect or to take note of; to look carefully, with attention to detail." Detective Sherlock Holmes was quick and correct to point out to his friend, "Watson, you see but you do not observe."

OBSERVATION

To inspect or to take note of Scripture; to look carefully,
with attention to detail

Louis Agassiz, a well-known nineteenth-century naturalist from Harvard, was asked, "What was your greatest contribution, scientifically?" Agassiz didn't hesitate: "I have taught men and women to observe." Yogi Berra got it right: "You can observe a lot by watching." We smile at that, but the truth is, we often fail to observe—and when we do, we regret it.

This point was driven home for me when I came across this true account of Sir William Osler, the distinguished professor of medicine at Oxford University in the first part of the twentieth century. A stickler for detail, he was determined that his medical students become keen observers beginning early in their training. On one occasion, before a classroom full of young, wide-eyed medical students, he placed a small jar containing human urine on his desk. He said, "I want all of you to understand that this bottle contains a sample for analysis. It's often possible by tasting it that you can determine the disease from which your patient suffers."

Suiting action to words, he stuck his finger into the urine and then put a finger into his mouth. Then he continued, "Now, I'm going to pass this bottle around, and I ask that you do exactly as I did."

Every student cringed. The bottle made its way from row to row, from student to student, as each one gingerly poked a finger into the urine and then bravely sampled its contents with a frown. When the container finally made it back to the professor's desk, he said, "You will now understand what I mean when I speak about details. Had you been observant, you would have seen that I put my *index finger* into the bottle, but I put my *middle finger* into my mouth."[7]

Most of us think we're better at observing than we really are. Here's a quick test to check your observation skills:

OBSERVATION TEST

---

1. Think of your spouse or a good friend. What exactly was this person wearing when you most recently spent time with him or her?

2. Which inscription does not appear on the back of a one-dollar bill: "In God we trust," "The Great Seal," or "*E pluribus unum*"? You've handled dollar bills all your life. Surely you will know this!

3. How many miles are on your car's odometer today?

4. Is your mother right-handed or left-handed? How about your father?

5. Was Moses an only child, or did he have siblings? If he had siblings, how many? (For the answer, see Numbers 26:59.)

6. Who traveled with Paul on his first missionary journey? (For the answer, see Acts 13:1-3.)

7. Do all four Gospels (Matthew, Mark, Luke, and John) include a record of Jesus' birth? If not, which ones don't? (For the answer, see Matthew 1 and Luke 1.)

8. What's the brand name of the stove in your kitchen?

9. How many steps lead to the second floor in your home? If not your home, how many steps are there in the building you work in or leading up to the door at your church?

10. What's the speed limit on the main road closest to your home?

How many questions did you get right? We're generally surprised by how many things we don't know when we observe them more carefully.

I recently thought about my observation skills when I was driving through a school zone at twenty miles an hour. I realized I didn't know what time the light starts to blink yellow and when it goes off, though I pass by hundreds of times in a given month. I see it, but I've never observed the details. Since then, I've begun to notice that the times change from one school zone area to another.

I need to explain the difference between observation and interpretation. Observing is not the same as interpreting. Inside our kitchen cabinet, Cynthia and I have a small prescription container. These words appear on the label: "Take with food." These are three simple words, but what exactly do they mean? When I looked at them yesterday, I imagined how a person from another culture might interpret that statement. Should I take the pill, break it up in my food, and swallow it while I'm eating my meal? That's exactly what it says! But we know, because of experience, that we're to take the medicine after a meal so our stomach won't be upset when the chemical enters. That's what the bottle means, but that's not what it says. What it *means* is the interpretation. Determining what the text of Scripture says is the step before determining what it means.

Let's look at Psalm 119:18 as an example. Put your thinking cap on, since this will require concentration.

Open my eyes to see
    the wonderful truths in your instructions.

If I were to make a list of observations, the first thing I would notice is that this verse is a prayer. In fact, as we have already learned, all but four verses in Psalm 119 represent a prayer. Note that this prayer contains one specific request. Do you see it? Look again: "Open my eyes to see." But the psalmist wasn't saying, "Let me see the image of the letters that form words." Rather, he was saying, "Let me see the wonderful truths that are here."

The psalmist was acknowledging that God's truths are wonderful. So his request was specific: "Lord, I come to You today, and I ask You to open my eyes as I unroll the scroll." That was how the Bible was read in the days of the psalmist. He was saying, in effect, "As I come across a section of the law and read it, I want to know fully and completely what it is saying." I would call this prayer our mandate to vigilant observation of God's Word.

OBSERVING THE WORDS AND THE CONTEXT

Carefully observing the text is always the first step of studying the Scriptures. With the psalmist's prayer on our lips, let's turn to the verse that we'll spend most of our time with in this chapter: Acts 1:8. If you're not familiar with your Bible, it would help to turn back to the two-page chart in the insert and notice that there are thirty-nine books in the Old Testament and twenty-seven books in the New Testament. The New Testament begins with the four Gospels: Matthew, Mark, Luke, and John. After the book of John, the second shelf displays the book of Acts. This historical book records the actions of those who carried the message of Jesus to the people of the known world. That's why the book also goes by the name the Acts of the Apostles.

Locate verse 8 in the first chapter of Acts—one of the most familiar and important verses in the New Testament.

> But you will receive power when the Holy Spirit has come upon you; and you shall be My witnesses both in Jerusalem, and in all Judea and Samaria, and even to the remotest part of the earth.
>
> ACTS 1:8, NASB

At this point we have merely read the words of the verse, but we haven't yet observed very carefully. This takes time and effort.

So let's dive in together. Initially, we pay attention to the terms. Our full attention is given to each word. Forget the time this takes—focus on one word at a time and read it as if for the first time. It may be tempting to say to yourself, *Oh, I've read this verse many times. I'm totally familiar with this; I need to go on to something more interesting.* But if you do, you'll miss some of the treasures buried under the surface. Even if you think you know the verse, there is much here you've never really observed. You must discipline yourself to examine each word closely.

The first word is *but*. We know that this term represents a contrast or a change of direction. If we're moving in one direction and a
"but" occurs, it indicates a turn. "But" means there's a change from
what has been going on to something that will now take place.

What does that term of contrast force us to do? It requires us to
look back and determine what the contrast is. This process is called
checking the context. We understand a verse of Scripture better
when we grasp its context—when we acquaint ourselves with the
surrounding verses. Every verse sits within a larger context. So surrounding this verse, something is happening that causes the writer
to begin this statement with *but*. To determine the context, we
must go back to verse 4, where Jesus is sitting with His disciples:

> Gathering them together, He commanded them not to leave
> Jerusalem, but to wait for what the Father had promised,
> "Which," He said, "you heard of from Me; for John baptized
> with water, but you will be baptized with the Holy Spirit not
> many days from now."
> So when they had come together, they were asking
> Him, saying, "Lord, is it at this time You are restoring the
> kingdom to Israel?" He said to them, "It is not for you to
> know times or epochs which the Father has fixed by His own
> authority; but . . ."
> ACTS 1:4-8, NASB

Now you have some context. Do you realize what we were doing
when we read verses 4-7? We were listening to a conversation. Jesus
spoke, the apostles responded, and He gave them a statement.
Then they asked a question, and He corrected their assumption. In
other words, the conversation is a dialogue between Jesus and His
closest followers. And in the middle of the dialogue, He said, essentially, "But hold on." This *but* in verse 8 is important.

Look at verse 7 again: "It is not for you to know times or epochs which the Father has fixed by His own authority." This statement refers to when Jesus will return and establish His Kingdom. Jesus was saying that since we don't know when all those events will happen in the future, something will play a significant role in our lives. This is the contrast.

Let me remind you: never isolate a verse from its context. When we seize isolated verses without having a bigger view of how they fit in with the rest of the passage, it leads to error, especially when verses are pulled out of context.

Years ago, I had the privilege of leading one of my fellow Marines to Christ. I left the island of Okinawa before he did, and when I was leaving for California, he said, "When you're in the San Francisco Bay area, would you please visit my folks? I know they'd love to meet you. I've written them all about you."

"Sure," I said. "I'd love to."

Being discharged is a time-consuming process. While waiting for the paperwork to go through, I had a Sunday free, so I gave his parents a call on the Saturday before. "Oh, we've heard about you," they said. "You're the religious man who's been influencing our son."

Well, that was a good start, wasn't it? Right away I was marked as a "religious man."

"We want you to go to church with us," they said.

They went to a liberal church—something I realized when we first walked into the vestibule. It was extremely colorful and artsy.

"Isn't this a wonderful place? The marble is so beautiful. Look at the pictures on the walls," they said to me.

I looked at the massive, beautiful portraits. There was a painting of Abraham Lincoln. Beside him, I saw another painting of Mahatma Gandhi. Then there was yet another of Socrates, and alongside him, one of Jesus of Nazareth, followed by another American president. At the bottom, written in gold lettering, were the words, "You are all the children of God." At first glance, everyone who admired those beautiful, framed works of art would think that all being portrayed were children of God. But this verse goes on to say, "For you are all children of God through faith in Christ Jesus" (Galatians 3:26).

Eek! The entire verse is saying something very different from what those first seven words quoted in the vestibule implied. When you use only a portion of a verse, you can easily miss some nuances that are quite important. As we take Acts 1:8 apart, we need to understand not only each word but also the broader context of the verse.

Let's return to verse 8 and move on to the next word, *you*. In English, we can't tell if the word is singular or plural. However, having just looked at verse 6, where Jesus is speaking to His apostles, we now know that the *you* has to be plural. So we could say "you apostles" or "you followers of Mine." Again, we are carefully observing Scripture to find our answers.

This brings us to the main verb, "will receive." Look at this phrase in your own Bible. Jesus was saying that they weren't going to *cause* something to happen; they were going to *receive* something. Next we look at whether the verb is in the past, present, or future tense. "Will receive" obviously means that this event is going to happen in the future. As we read the verse, we can assume that the apostles didn't have the power then, but that a time would come in the future when they would receive it. Making this observation is not complicated, but if you skimmed the text, you might overlook it.

Most people read their Bible in a hurry so they can get through an entire chapter in ten or fifteen minutes. But if you wish to become a serious student of the Bible, you need to forget your speed-reading course. There's no rush.

Now is a good time to pause and summarize our observations thus far.

But[1] you[2] will receive[3] power when the Holy Spirit has come upon you; and you shall be My witnesses both in Jerusalem, and in all Judea and Samaria, and even to the remotest part of the earth.

[1] **(But)** This is a contrast from what was previously stated.

[2] **(you)** This is a plural pronoun referring to Jesus' apostles.

[3] **(will receive)** This is future tense, because they do not currently have the power.

If it's important enough for Jesus to say "But you will receive," it's important enough for us to discover what He's referring to. Receive *what*? He uses the word "power." If we look up this word in the dictionary, we find this definition: "the ability or capacity to act or perform effectively." *Power* is a significant word in the verse and therefore deserves investigation. This is a good time to observe the cause-and-effect nature of Jesus' statement: "You will receive power when the Holy Spirit has come upon you."

Now, stop and picture the scene. The apostles aren't praying for the Holy Spirit. They're not trying to bargain, thinking that if they give up something, they'll get the Holy Spirit in return. They're not promising that they're going to be living good, clean lives so the Holy Spirit will come to them. No, Jesus says simply, "You will receive." This is a promise. In fact, it's an unconditional promise. In a sense, He's saying, "You can count on this. You're going to receive power because it will come from the Holy Spirit." The Spirit of God is the cause, and the effect is the presence of His power in their lives.

And that's not the only promise here. Look at the next term: the small connective *and*. "And you shall be My witnesses." I marked both *will* and *shall* in my Bible. You *will* receive power, and at the same time, you *shall* tell the story. Jesus said they would receive power and they would be His witnesses. Both these promises are straight from Him.

As I observe more and more details, I pause and allow my imagination to run free. I try to picture those men as they heard what was being said. How amazed and excited they must have been! You know why? Because in the previous setting, when the apostles were with Jesus, they were running away after His arrest. He was going on trial and would ultimately be nailed to a cross. These same men who ran away had now returned to Him. They'd seen Him, they'd heard Him say, "Don't be afraid." They'd received His assurance. And now, of all things, they were being told, *You're not going to be punished for running away. As a matter of fact, something transformational is going to happen in your lives. You're going to receive power from the Holy Spirit—the third member of the Trinity. You're going to have supernatural strength. You're going to have insight into the truth of My Word. You're going to have courage. You won't be intimidated when opponents stand against you.*

See the benefit of using the imagination? We can allow words to paint the scene. We enter into their world and consider what it must have been like to have heard Jesus say to us, along with the apostles, "You're going to receive power, and you're going to tell people about Him, as His witnesses everywhere!" Our tendency may be to begin to apply what we've learned right away, but we're going to force ourselves to continue observing for now.

The verse doesn't end before Jesus gets specific about location. Where will the apostles go when they witness? Observe the end of verse 8: "In Jerusalem, and in all Judea and Samaria, and even to the remotest part of the earth."

This should cue us to ask ourselves, *Where are those places?* When locations are mentioned in the Bible, we need to find them on a map. As it turns out, all those places were located in the land of Israel. Open your atlas or turn to the back of your

Bible and find your maps. You should have a map titled "The Ministry of Jesus" or something similar. Examine the map. Take time to familiarize yourself with the land of Israel (often called Palestine) in Jesus' day. At the top of the map is a body of water called the Sea of Galilee. Toward the bottom is a much larger body of water called the Dead Sea. Running north to south between is the Jordan River, which flows out of the Sea of Galilee and into the Dead Sea. To find Jerusalem, go to the northern part of the Dead Sea and then look to the west. There you'll find the city of Jerusalem—the "home base" for the apostles. Jesus said they would be His witnesses right there in Jerusalem. After being empowered, they would start where they were. Fix that fact in your mind.

Next Jesus promises that they would be His witnesses in Judea. Look for large letters near Jerusalem that say "Judea." Judea was a province, which is similar to a state in the United States. Jerusalem was a city located in the province of Judea, just like Dallas is in the "province" of Texas. Jesus was saying that not only would the disciples be witnesses for Him in their own city; they'd also take the message to cities around them—to places located in the province of Judea.

To find Samaria, move your finger north. Look for the word in the same size print as Judea since it, too, is a province.

Jesus was telling His apostles that *when they received power, they would be His witnesses where they lived and then outside where they lived, and they'd even take His message to Samaria. And from there, they'd carry it to the remotest part of the earth.*

That last phrase—"to the remotest part of the earth"—is such broad geography that the map on the ministry of Jesus doesn't cover it. If you find a map that traces the journeys of Paul, you will see how the message began to spread throughout the book of Acts.

Let's return to our key verse, Acts 1:8. I want to tie this together

ROMAN DIVISION OF PALESTINE

ABILENE

ITUREA

Sidon

Damascus   Abana R.

SYRIA

Mt. Hermon ▲

Coastal Road

PHOENICIA

Caesarea Philippi

TRACONITIS

Tyre

Litani R.

Cadasa (Kedesh)

Lake Hula

GALILEE

Mt. Meron ▲

GAULANITIS

Ptolemais (Acco)

Korazin

Capernaum

Bethsaida

Sea of Galilee (Kinnereth)

BATANEA

Mediterranean Sea (Great Sea)

Mt. Carmel ▲

Kishon R.

Tiberias

Mt. Tabor ▲

Yarmuk R.

Gadara ○

AURANITIS

Caesarea

Great Trunk Road

Scythopolis (Beth-shan) ○

DECAPOLIS

SAMARIA

Jordan R.

Sebaste (Samaria)

Mt. Ebal ▲

Yarkon R.

Sychar (Shechem)

Mt. Gerizim ▲

Jabbok R.

Antipatris (Aphek)

Joppa

PEREA

Bethel

Ephraim

Tyrus ●

Philadelphia (Amman) ○

Azotus (Ashdod)

Mt. of Olives

Jerusalem

Jericho ■

Cyprus ■

Bethany

Esbus (Heshbon) ■

Bethlehem

JUDEA

Herodium ■

Gaza

Hebron

Dead Sea (Salt Sea)

NABATEA

En-gedi

Arnon R.

IDUMEA

Masada ■

King's Highway

Beersheba

Besor Brook

Division of Herod's kingdom to his three sons

- Territory of Archelaus
- Territory of Herod Antipas
- Territory of Philip
- Territory of the Proconsul of Syria
- Extent of Herod the Great's kingdom

● City
○ Decapolis city
■ Herodian fortress
▲ Mountain peak

0   10   20 Miles
0   10   20 Kilometers

35°E   36°E

33°N

32°N

31°N

in a way that may surprise you. What we have here in Acts 1:8 is an inspired outline of the entire book of Acts. For the first seven chapters, the apostles were in *Jerusalem*, witnessing, suffering, and enduring intense persecution. The apostles and leaders of the early church were misunderstood by the religious community, and some of them were facing harassment and arrest. At the same time, they were watching God bless them as their numbers increased. Their empowered ministry in Jerusalem begins in Acts 2 and continues through chapter 7.

As a result of the intense persecution, the apostles were forced to scatter, and they moved out into *Judea* (Acts 8). In Acts 9, Paul (originally named Saul) was converted while on his way to Damascus. His plan had been to intimidate and silence the Christians living there, but God had other plans! After his conversion and transformation, he took the message far beyond Judea to the Gentile world. So between Acts chapter 8 and the end of the book, Paul and others went into *Samaria* and ultimately to *the remotest part of the world.*

If you had asked people in that day to identify the farthest part of the world, most would have named Rome, where the emperor and the Roman government were located. And would you believe that before the end of Paul's life, he had a face-to-face audience with the emperor? That entire flow of events is exactly what Jesus promised in Acts 1:8. He literally outlined the itinerary of the spread of the gospel!

Sometimes it's helpful to try and summarize the text in your own words to enhance your understanding. Another glance into Acts 1 prompts this loose rendering of Jesus' words to His close followers:

But since I'm not able to give you the specific time of My return to this earth, let Me tell you what will happen in the meantime.

You're going to be the recipients of invincible, divine power—
power that will be sourced in the Holy Spirit. He will fill you
with His power so you will become transformed individuals.
You will no longer operate out of fear and insecurity and
intimidation. You will instead carry My message into this very
city and then into the province around it. You will carry My
message into Samaria, in places you've never been. You will
become God-inspired spokespersons. And then from there, you will
take it everywhere—into the far-reaching realms of the earth.

But[1] you[2] will receive[3] **power**[4] when the Holy Spirit has come upon you; and you shall be My **witnesses**[5] both in **Jerusalem**, and in all **Judea** and **Samaria**, and even to the **remotest part of the earth**[6].

[1] **(But)** This is a contrast from what was previously stated.

[2] **(you)** This is a plural pronoun referring to Jesus' apostles.

[3] **(will receive)** This is future tense, because they do not currently have the power.

[4] **(power)** The power comes from the Holy Spirit.

[5] **(witnesses)** The power is for witnessing.

[6] **(Jerusalem, Judea, Samaria, and the remotest part of the earth)** The witnesses move from where they are across the entire world.

I need to pause here to express my excitement! Think about what Jesus predicted—think of the incredible hope and encouragement that must have flooded over His disciples. What is so remarkable is that all of these insights have come from just the first step in "preparing the meal." We've simply *observed* what's packed in one verse—that beats preparing the ingredients for making a cake by a long shot!

So right about now you may be feeling a little smug. "Hey, I know this verse. Look at all these observations we've made. I'm ready to roll!" I remember that feeling from when I took one of Dr. Hendricks's courses called Bible Study Methods, back when I was in my first year at seminary. All of us students were perched on the edges of our seats. No teacher was like Prof Hendricks when he taught his students how to study the Bible. I clearly remember him saying, "All right, men"—back in 1959, only men attended Dallas Theological Seminary—"when you go home to your dorm or your apartment tonight, I want you to write down fifty observations from Acts 1:8 on a sheet of paper." My first thought was, *You've got to be kidding. Fifty? I figured I'd be doing well to list ten or twelve.* That night I sat down in our little apartment, and after a considerable amount of time, I wrote down fifty observations. I was feeling pretty special when I brought it back to class the next day. After we all laid our fifty observations in front of him, he said, "Good work. Now go home tonight and find fifty more from the same verse." My jaw hit my chest! Was he kidding? But guess what? We did it. How is that possible?

The answer is simple: we have an *infinite text*! The Bible is unfathomable. Its truths are beyond measurement. You could take another verse of Scripture or a section of Scripture and keep yourself busy for hours. How? By doing just what we've been doing: digging into the words, observing the context, examining the details, and seeing how they relate to each other.

A FEAST FOR THE SENSES

Enjoying a delicious meal is always a feast for the senses. How the meal looks and smells, along with the texture and the taste, makes the food delightful. It's the same with the Scriptures. As we learn to engage our senses, the verses come alive in our minds . . . and ultimately in our lives! This process begins when we learn to see what we're reading.

Let's begin with the eyes. In order to become astute observers, we need to read as if for the first time. When we train ourselves to see God's Word with fresh eyes, chances are good that we'll notice details we've never seen there before. Seriously!

Several years ago I was riding with our youngest son in his pickup truck, and we were following a large white FedEx truck. We were talking about other topics, not about the truck, when Chuck suddenly interrupted our conversation. "See the arrow?"

"Arrow?"

"Yeah, that arrow on the FedEx truck logo—see it?"

"Are we looking at the same truck?" I asked.

"Yeah, Dad, *look*!"

I couldn't figure out what he was saying. "What arrow?"

He laughed. "That white arrow between the *e* and the *x*."

I stared and studied the logo. All of a sudden I saw it. I had never seen the arrow in the logo before, even though I'd been around those trucks for years. But now, every time I look at a FedEx truck, all I can see is that arrow! It's funny how once you've discovered something, you wonder how you could have overlooked it for so long.

As you begin to reacquaint yourself with the Scriptures, you will make numerous observations for the first time. They've been there all along, but suddenly your eyes will see truths you've missed all your life. One method that will help you make original and insightful observations is to look at a Bible version that's different from the one you normally use. For this study, I pulled my copy of *The Message* from my shelf and turned to Acts 1:8. Eugene Peterson renders the verse this way:

He told them, "You don't get to know the time. Timing is the Father's business. What you'll get is the Holy Spirit. And when the Holy Spirit comes on you, you will be able to be

my witnesses in Jerusalem, all over Judea and Samaria, even
to the ends of the world."

ACTS 1:7-8, MSG

The meaning is similar here, but there's some helpful amplification.
When we're serious about the Scriptures, we read other versions to
give us a broader understanding. I never prepare a message without
taking the time to read other versions. Invariably, that helps me see
the words as if for the first time.

Here's another tip: pay attention to the sounds in the Scriptures.
Can you hear the sounds of vegetables being chopped or the sizzle
of a steak on a grill while preparing a meal? I suggest that you start
reading your Bible with your ears—as if you're reading a love letter.
Listen to the words, and feel the emotions. I remember when I was
overseas for more than sixteen months, far from my wife. When I
got a love letter from her, I would never say, "Oh, it's just another
letter from Cynthia. That's nice," and then go about my work. Are
you kidding? I'd say, "Whoa!" And then there's the "smell test." *Ah,
man! It smells just like her fragrance. Yeah, that's her. Wow!*

In one letter she began, "Dear Charles" (she used to call me
Charles). However, in her previous letter she began, "My dearest
darling Charles." But this time she wrote simply, "Dear Charles."
*Why the change? What does that mean? What happened? Was some-
thing different?* Remember, when you're reading a love letter, there's
no such thing as an insignificant word. I retreated to a quiet,
private place, and I read her words aloud so my ears could hear
what my mouth was saying. And I could hear her voice through
the lines. I should add that I read them repeatedly. Some letters
I read eight, ten, maybe twelve times. All I had from her were
her love letters to me. They always told me more than just facts
and events. They included words of affection. They meant something extremely important to me because I was in a lonely place,

surrounded by fellow Marines but far from home. I drained every ounce of my wife's emotion from each letter I received. I entered into her world. I allowed her words to simmer on the back burner of my mind. I lived for her love letters!

So read the Bible as God's love letter to you. Read the words repeatedly. Read them aloud. If you were in my study, you would hear me having conversations with God about what He has written. I talk to Him, and I interact with His words. That's the way I get to know the Scriptures—and the way to know God! That's why when I teach a passage of Scripture, it's as if I've been there before. I have relived the scene—heard the crackle of the fire, smelled the fish Jesus was grilling by the shore, tasted the bread He served His disciples. I repeat: going through this process takes time. Maybe you have only thirty minutes a day. Then observe what you're reading for thirty minutes a day.

The third way you need to read the Bible is with your nose. You need the nose of a detective. Think of television shows that include crime-scene investigations. Detectives study every hair, every thread, every hint, every smudge, every recorded phone conversation, every e-mail message, and every smell. Keen-minded detectives look carefully at each handprint, fingerprint, and shoeprint. Detectives know that every clue they look for says something important. So when you search the Scriptures, pay attention to verbs, nouns, prepositions, adjectives, adverbs, and even pronouns. You might think, *Pronouns? What's the big deal?*

Let's turn to Acts 16, and we'll discover the importance of pronouns. Acts 16 is a record of Paul's second missionary journey. Paul has waited for the Lord to guide him and his companions, but no opportunities have opened up. He has attempted to preach at different places, but all the doors have been slammed shut.

That night Paul had a vision: A man from Macedonia in northern Greece was standing there, pleading with him,

"Come over to Macedonia and help us!" So we decided to
leave for Macedonia at once, having concluded that God was
calling us to preach the Good News there.

We boarded a boat at Troas and sailed straight across to
the island of Samothrace, and the next day we landed at
Neapolis. From there we reached Philippi, a major city of
that district of Macedonia and a Roman colony. And we
stayed there several days.

ACTS 16:9-12

The first part of this account says Paul has a vision (verse 9). The
pronoun *us* at the end of verse 9 ("help us") refers to the people of
Macedonia. Look at the next pronoun at the beginning of verse 10:
"So we." Let's stop and think. Not "they," but "we." For the first
time in Acts, the person writing the book of Acts (Luke) enters
into the narrative himself. At this point, Luke joins the travelers.
It's not just Paul or Silas or the other companions but Luke as well.
Sometimes the account reads "they" and "them"; other times it
says "we" and "us," alerting the reader of those times when Luke is
included.

When you have the nose of a detective, you'll notice many of
these little details that turn out to be significant. And when you
point them out to those you're teaching, they'll love the discoveries
they make! It's amazing what we can learn from carefully observing
the text. The man who wrote the book of Acts wasn't engaged in
any of the journeys until chapter 16. And from then on, Luke plays
a very significant role as Paul's companion and personal physician.

Think of your favorite meal, perfectly prepared. Imagine the
taste as the first bite touches your tongue. Magnificent! It's the
same with God's Word. When we carefully study the Bible, we
have the privilege of tasting the text. Read the text as if you are in
it. I try to imagine what it must have been like to be in the crowd

when Jesus walked through. I put myself on the sick bed and try
to picture what it must have been like not to be able to walk and
then, suddenly, having the ability to stand up and move around.
There is a remarkable feeling that comes over me as a result of
entering into the text myself. You can have the same experience. It's
exhilarating!

I'll take all this one step further. If you're going to study the
book of 1 Corinthians, join the church in Corinth. Imagine what it
was like to be a church that was filled with conflict and disruptive
schism. If you're going to read and study the Resurrection, walk
into the tomb! Stand alongside Peter and John, and experience
that eerie moment when you're looking at wrappings that are still
in the shape of a body but flattened, with no body inside. Imagine
what those men must have thought: *What does all this mean?* When
you're with Isaiah in chapter 6, stand beside him when he sees the
Lord high and holy and lifted up, and when he hears the angel
saying, "Holy, holy, holy is the Lord of Heaven's Armies" (verse
3). Feel the chill down your spine! Listen to the angels as they
flap their wings while surrounding God in His throne room, then
repeat the words of praise yourself. When I taught this passage in
a sermon, I had the congregation sound forth, shouting repeatedly, "Holy, holy, holy! Holy, holy, holy!" How did I think of doing
that? It happened in my study, when I was sitting at my desk and
saying the words. I was thinking, *How can I get this idea across?*
And then it occurred to me: *I'll have everybody enter into the text
and become one of the seraphim.*

Isaiah's response to the awesome holiness of God was a wave of
guilt and shame over his sin. One of the seraphim took a burning
coal from the altar with a pair of tongs and touched Isaiah's lips.
Can you feel the burn of the hot coal on your mouth? When we
use this approach of observing with our senses, the Bible becomes
alive and active!

FIVE SIGNALS TO LOOK FOR

Before ending this chapter, I have one more important suggestion to help you become an astute observer of the Scriptures. This tip has several parts. First, find a pen and paper. Then trace your hand—around your thumb and then around each finger down to the wrist on each side. This will help you remember the five signals to look for. We're going to write labels on the thumb and each of the four fingers.

1. **First, write the word *emphasized* on the thumb.** When you look at your Bible, always look for what is emphasized. How do you know what is being emphasized? By the amount of space being used to discuss and explain it. Genesis is about Creation, and it's about the Fall. And then it's about the beginning of nations. And then it's all about Abraham. Abraham's story is told in Genesis 12–27, and the amount of space tells you that he's the one being emphasized. So, starting with your thumb, remember: emphasized themes.

2. **On the index finger, write the word *repeated.*** These are words that are used frequently in the Bible. Remember when we looked at the first section of the book of Proverbs in chapter 2? The phrase "my child" was repeated over and over. The writer of Proverbs repeated these words because he was offering counsel to his son. Notice particularly when a name is mentioned twice, as in "Abraham! Abraham! . . . Don't lay a hand on the boy!" (Genesis 22:11-12) or "Saul! Saul! Why are you persecuting me?" (Acts 9:4). A repetition of the same name means, "This is important!" Often the repetition is intended to build to a climax. Think of your index finger as your "pointer." This will remind you to point out repeated words.

3. **On the middle finger, write the word *related*.** Look for ideas in Scripture that are closely connected. Here's how they typically appear: questions are followed by answers. We've seen an example of this in Acts 1:7-9. Promises are followed by rewards; warnings are followed by failure or obedience; sin is usually followed by consequences. Take note of terms or expressions that are closely related to one another, because they will show you the correct meaning of the passage.

4. **On the ring finger, write the word *alike*.** Ideas that are alike are sometimes introduced with "as" and followed by "so." Look at a few examples:

   "As the deer longs for streams of water, so I long for you, O God" (Psalm 42:1). What a beautiful word picture. These are things that are alike. The words "as" and "so" are introducing analogies. We who thirst for God's truth are like deer in a forest, searching for and being satisfied by fresh water from a bubbling brook. Here are other examples that don't use "as" and "so" but still show two things that are similar:

   "I am the vine; you are the branches" (John 15:5).

   "We are the clay, and you are the potter" (Isaiah 64:8).

5. **Finally, on the smallest finger, write the word *unlike*.** This has to do with opposites. There is a sharp contrast between the list of attributes that describe the sinful nature (Galatians 5:19-21) and the fruit of the Spirit list that follows (5:22-23). The contrast between the two lists shows that one is unlike the other. Paul is showing that the believer who has the Holy Spirit is completely opposite from the unbeliever. The contrast forces us to choose one side or the other.

Even if we have been given the gift of sight, we're not given the gift of observation until the Lord steps in and enlightens our minds. As we give ourselves to the words of Scripture through prayer and time and discipline, we'll begin to hear things we've never heard before and we'll see things we've never seen. As God's Word comes to life, we will find ourselves thrilled beyond words!

There's a key to unlocking insights into the Bible. Clara Scott, who wrote the words of this hymn, had that truth in mind:

> *Open my eyes, that I may see*
> *glimpses of truth thou hast for me. . . .*
> *Open my ears, that I may hear.*

Finally she says,

> *Place in my hands the wonderful key*
> *That shall unclasp and set me free.*

The key is observation. Just as healthy, wholesome cooking begins with a careful consideration of the ingredients, effective Bible study starts with careful observation.

> > Start prayerfully.
> > Go slowly.
> > Read carefully.
> > Think deeply.
> > Feel passionately.

Think of these steps as rungs on a pantry ladder that help you reach the top shelf. We are well on our way to that delicious feast. I can almost smell the sweet aroma coming from the kitchen.

YOUR TURN IN THE KITCHEN

Reading the ingredients in a recipe is a careful process—one that's critical for ensuring that a meal turns out right. Similarly, it's helpful to develop your observation skills as you're studying the Scriptures. Here are several exercises for you to try:

1. One of the ways you can hone your general observation skills is by using all of your senses. Go to a familiar public place, such as a coffee shop, and sit there for thirty minutes. During that time, write down only the new observations you make about that place. Record everything you observe through your five senses (sight, hearing, smell, taste, and touch). What did you observe that you never noticed before? What did you learn about the power of observation?

2. Look up John 3:16 in your own Bible. Take time to read all of chapter 3 to understand the context. In your journal or on a piece of paper, write down twenty-five observations from John 3:16 (similar to what we did for Acts 1:8).

3. While observation begins with an individual verse, it's important to observe a passage of Scripture in context. This skill will be useful whether you're studying God's Word on your own or preparing a lesson or sermon. Slowly and carefully read Philippians 4:4-9, and then write down twenty key observations. Take your time, following the instructions from this chapter.

4. It's important to observe the teachings of Jesus because they provide a foundation for our faith. One of Jesus' most common teaching methods was to tell parables or short stories to present and explain His point. Read the parable of the Good Samaritan in Luke 10:25-37. Then make ten observations about what you see in this parable and its context. Pay close attention to what prompted Jesus to tell this story.

5. The Bible is full of stories where God interacts with people and nations. Learning how to observe a narrative well is important in both studying and teaching the Scriptures. Carefully read the story about Daniel in the lions' den in Daniel 6:1-28. Then make ten observations about this true account.

6. Practice using your imagination to picture a biblical scene in your head. Carefully read Isaiah 6:1-8, and then describe how the seraphim might have looked. How might Isaiah have felt? Use the five senses (sight, hearing, smell, taste, and touch) to describe the scene. How does creating this scene in your imagination affect your understanding of it and your ability to communicate it?

Additional tip: Develop a marking system in your Bible for observing the Scriptures. For instance, you could draw a box around connecting words (*and*, *but*, *therefore*, *since*); underline promises; and write "def" in the margin when you come to a word that is defined in the verse (such as faith, which is defined in Hebrews 11:1). Write down your system and use it consistently when you study the Scriptures. You may wish to use colored pens to mark words and/or verses in your Bible. Colors can help you emphasize certain words you want to remember. For example, you might want to underscore important commands in red or circle prominent names in blue or highlight significant questions in yellow. The possibilities are endless. Just remember to be consistent with your system.

CHAPTER 5

UNDERSTANDING THE NUTRIENTS

Interpreting the Text

A FEAST THAT IS BOTH TASTY AND HEALTHY requires a lot from the chef. He or she must understand not only the taste of the flavors but also the nutrients the meal provides. Certain flavors complement one another well, while others don't. Some foods contain many calories but don't provide lasting nutrition for the body. For a meal to be healthy and enjoyable, it needs to include a balance of both flavorful ingredients and beneficial nutrients. A good chef works diligently to put nutritious, delicious meals together.

Just like those who handle food wisely and well, we as followers of Christ need to cultivate skills for handling the Word of God responsibly and accurately. The Bible is not a code book reserved for the most advanced scholars. It doesn't contain secret messages hidden on the page. God's Word was written for ordinary people—like you and me—to help us understand His will and walk in His ways. But as we're discovering, preparing a nutritious meal from the Scriptures doesn't come quickly or naturally. No one is born with an innate ability to understand the truth of God, even after becoming a Christian. The acquisition of knowledge and understanding comes as a result of the work of the Spirit in a person's life.

In this process of learning how to handle the Bible responsibly, we're learning that we need to practice and refine certain disciplines. I've spent my life developing these disciplines—and I continue to do so. My hope in sharing these insights with you is that you might begin to do the same. My basic task as a pastor is to be a faithful expositor of the Scriptures and, in doing so, to equip God's people to do the work of ministry on their own. This is precisely what Paul was saying in Ephesians 4:12: "[The pastors'] responsibility is to equip God's people to do his work and build up the church, the body of Christ." We need guidance from the Holy Scriptures to do His work.

As we've discussed in previous chapters, in order to learn and apply truths from God's Word, we must follow certain guidelines. As with preparing a gourmet meal, we need to follow an intentional process if we're to create a delicious outcome. Let's take a moment to review the four steps we must take in searching the Scriptures:

1. **The first step is observation.** Observation answers the question "What does the Bible say?" If we read a novel, we're first observing what it says. If we read an article from a magazine, we observe the words that form sentences. Then we read the paragraphs so that we might discover the writer's purpose.

2. **The second step is interpretation.** This is true whether we're reading a novel, a magazine article, a verse of Scripture, an

e-mail message, or a note from a friend. We must embrace this step to grasp the meaning. Interpretation is understanding what the Bible means.

3. **This third step is called correlation.** At this stage, we're focusing on the question "What does the Bible say elsewhere about this topic?" As you are learning how to interpret, it's necessary to check other verses that address the same subject. No verse in the Bible is isolated. No truth stands by itself. Just as the diamond in a ring has a setting, so every verse of Scripture has a broader context. By comparing the verse with other verses, we gain a deeper understanding of what it means. For example, when reading the story of the Ethiopian eunuch in Acts 8, we discover that he was struggling to understand the identity of the person mentioned in Isaiah 53. We are wise to turn from Acts 8 to the words of the prophet Isaiah so we can grasp the bigger picture. In other words, we correlate or compare those two passages.

4. **The fourth step is the crowning part of the process: application.** This is when we ask, "What does the Bible mean for me personally or for someone else?" Here we consider how the Scriptures relate to where we work or go to school, how to get along with a difficult person, and how to deal with challenges in marriage, with children, or with parents. What does the Bible have to say about decisions we need to make? What about a struggle with a certain disease? How can we stay strong through pain? The Bible addresses all areas of life.

When we apply what we've observed, interpreted, and correlated, Scripture bursts to life! The process may sound tedious and complicated, but it's neither. As we learn the steps together, it will become a natural habit every time you come to Scripture. Even if this is new information for you, it isn't difficult to grasp once you learn each step in the process.

WHAT DOES IT ALL MEAN?

We'll be focusing on the second step of Bible study for the remainder of this chapter: *interpretation*. What does this step refer to? Very simply, it's coming to an understanding of what the Bible means. I have interpreted the Bible for you when I have explained to you what the words and sentences are teaching. Once you have taught yourself the correct techniques involved in interpreting the Scriptures, you won't need others to tell you. If you know the Lord Jesus Christ, you have all the equipment necessary for you to do your own meal preparation and cooking.

INTERPRETATION

Coming to an understanding of what the Bible means

As you dig in and discover biblical truths on your own, you will realize that interpretation is both a science and an art. It's a science because it's guided by rules that form a system. When you know and follow those rules, you'll begin to interpret Scripture accurately. You'll guard against error, and you'll gain discernment. You'll be able to spot false messages, whether written or spoken. You'll become more stable in your faith; you'll be able to stand on your own as you master the science of interpretation. But interpretation is also an art, in that it requires Spirit-directed skill to follow these rules as you interpret the Bible. We'll get into this in more depth later in this chapter.

It's important to note here what interpretation is *not*, which is as important as understanding what it is. Interpretation is not the same as imposing your opinions on the Bible. You might have been taught something all your life that is incorrect, and you find yourself looking for proof in the Bible. That's not interpretation; that's trying to verify what someone has told you. Interpretation is drawing out what the text says and what it means. It's what you glean from the Bible itself. Furthermore, interpretation isn't based on the way you feel. Some days I don't feel good at all, yet I'm engaged in the study of the Scriptures. My emotions or physical well-being may affect my ability to concentrate, but the Scriptures speak for themselves. Correct interpretation isn't based on wanting the text to say what we have in mind. It's learning what it actually means, based on what it says.

To illustrate how dependent we are on God to arrive at a correct interpretation, let's turn to Psalm 119 again. Verse 27 says,

Help me understand the meaning of your commandments,
and I will meditate on your wonderful deeds.

The verse opens with this prayer: "Help me understand." These are words of dependence. I don't know how many times in my Christian life I've prayed simply, "Help me, O Lord." "Help me make the best decision." "Help me get through this difficult period of testing." "Help me as I face a situation I'm not familiar with." Or this frequent request: "Help me as I lead this flock." Often I pray, "Help me understand the meaning of your commandments." These are prayers of dependence. To interpret the Bible well, we must pray for understanding.

Look further and ponder the words of verses 33-34:

Teach me your decrees, O Lord;
I will keep them to the end.

Give me understanding and I will obey your instructions;
   I will put them into practice with all my
      heart.

PSALM 119:33-34

Verse 33 opens with the words "Teach me," and verse 34 begins
with "Give me." One after another, we see what the psalmist is
asking of God. It would be a great study to read through this
psalm and list the requests he asks of God. That would reveal
what the psalm teaches about prayer. By digging into each
verse, we would begin to discern the depth of meaning in each
prayer.

Now let's turn to the New Testament book of Acts, where we
find a captivating story in the middle of chapter 8. This account
involves two people who couldn't be more different from each
other. One is an evangelist named Philip, and the other is an
Ethiopian eunuch, whose name is not revealed. We do know that
he is the treasurer of Ethiopia and that he has been in Jerusalem
for worship. By the providence of God, the two men are brought
together. Look at what transpired:

As for Philip, an angel of the Lord said to him, "Go
south down the desert road that runs from Jerusalem
to Gaza."

ACTS 8:26

Incidentally, I should warn you not to wait for an angel to say
something like this to you! The reason it happened in the days
of the early church is because the Bible wasn't completed yet,
so God revealed Himself in some unusual ways—including
through the instruction of angelic beings, visions, and dreams.
In this case, the angel literally told Philip to go south along the

112

desert road to Gaza. Today, far too many people are waiting for a voice from heaven or looking to the sky for some cloud-formed message or listening late at night for the whisper of God. God doesn't usually speak to us in those ways. He talks to us in His Word. His message to us today is this: "Read My Word. It's all there."

According to verse 25, Philip had been in Samaria. We might think of Philip as the Billy Graham of the first century. He ministered during some very exciting times, and as he delivered the message of the gospel, people in various parts of Samaria trusted in Christ. In the midst of his evangelizing, the Lord said to him, in effect, "Philip, your work here is finished. I want you to go down a desert road." There was no wrestling match between Philip and the Lord. As we'll read in verse 27, Philip went immediately.

Philip's journey took him toward Gaza—a place you may not be familiar with. If your Bible has maps, look for a map that covers the ministry of Jesus. (Gaza doesn't appear on every map, so you may have to check more than one source.) On the map, locate a small body of water called the Sea of Galilee to the north and the Dead Sea to the south. With your finger, trace the Jordan River from the Sea of Galilee to the Dead Sea. When you get to the top of the Dead Sea, move your finger west (left) until you find Jerusalem. Gaza is southwest of Jerusalem, just off the coast of the Mediterranean Sea. Philip started in Samaria and then went from Jerusalem to Gaza. That's a long trek to a lonely desert area, especially since there aren't many towns or cities between Jerusalem and Gaza. The Judean wilderness was a barren place, with few blades of grass and hardly a bush or a shrub in sight. Philip must have wondered why he was to go there.

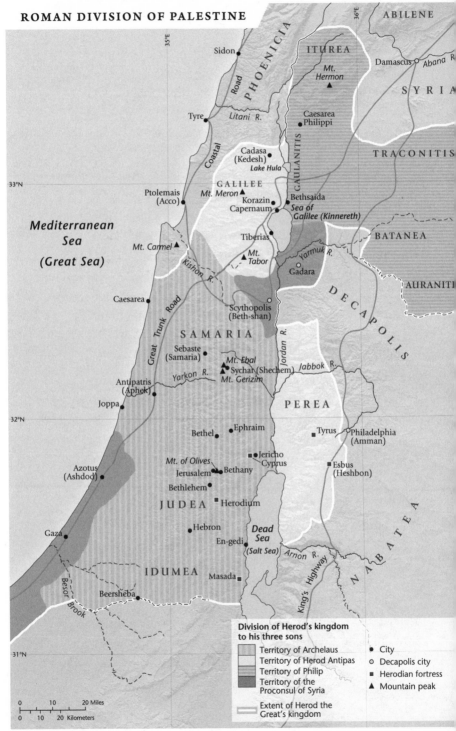

ROMAN DIVISION OF PALESTINE

ABILENE

Sidon

PHOENICIA

ITUREA

Damascus · Abana R.

SYRIA

Mt. Hermon ▲

Coastal Road

Tyre

Litani R.

Caesarea Philippi ●

GAULANITIS

TRACONITIS

33°N

Cadasa (Kedesh) ●

Lake Hula

GALILEE

Ptolemais (Acco) ●

Mt. Meron ▲

Korazin ●

Capernaum ●

● Bethsaida

Sea of Galilee (Kinnereth)

BATANEA

Mediterranean Sea (Great Sea)

Mt. Carmel ▲

Tiberias ●

Kishon R.

Mt. Tabor ▲

Yarmuk R.

Gadara ○

AURANITIS

Caesarea ●

Great Trunk Road

Scythopolis (Beth-shan) ○

D E C A P O L I S

SAMARIA

Sebaste (Samaria) ●

Mt. Ebal ▲

Sychar (Shechem) ●

Mt. Gerizim ▲

Jordan R.

Jabbok R.

Yarkon R.

Antipatris (Aphek) ●

Joppa ●

P E R E A

32°N

Bethel ●

Ephraim ●

Tyrus ■

Philadelphia (Amman) ○

Mt. of Olives

Jericho ●

Azotus (Ashdod) ●

Jerusalem ■ ● Bethany

Cyprus ●

Esbus (Heshbon) ■

Bethlehem ●

JUDEA

■ Herodium

N A B A T E A

Gaza ●

Hebron ●

Dead Sea (Salt Sea)

En-gedi ●

IDUMEA

Masada ■

Arnon R.

King's Highway

Beersheba ●

Besor Brook

31°N

Division of Herod's kingdom to his three sons

Territory of Archelaus
Territory of Herod Antipas
Territory of Philip
Territory of the Proconsul of Syria

Extent of Herod the Great's kingdom

● City
○ Decapolis city
■ Herodian fortress
▲ Mountain peak

0   10   20 Miles
0   10   20 Kilometers

So why did he? Look at Acts 8 again, and let's see how the Lord works:

> So he started out, and he met the treasurer of Ethiopia, a eunuch of great authority under the Kandake, the queen of Ethiopia. The eunuch had gone to Jerusalem to worship, and he was now returning. Seated in his carriage, he was reading aloud from the book of the prophet Isaiah.
>
> ACTS 8:27-28

We serve a God who is Lord over the entire universe, which means that no one is a stranger to Him. God sovereignly led an Ethiopian eunuch into that barren wilderness on his way back to Ethiopia. God knew exactly where he was and where he was going—and that he'd have to go through Gaza to get there. There's nowhere you can go outside the Lord's awareness. The prophet Isaiah addresses the Lord's ever-present interest in our lives:

> Can a mother forget her nursing child?
>   Can she feel no love for the child she has borne?
> But even if that were possible,
>   I would not forget you!
> See, I have written your name on the palms of my hands.
>
> ISAIAH 49:15-16

Your location is as clear to the Lord as the nose on your face. God knows exactly where you are. He knew where the Ethiopian eunuch was. He knew that this man needed to talk to Philip, and He knew that Philip had the Good News the man needed to hear. So God sent Philip all the way there to be with the eunuch.

The Ethiopian man was riding along, reading from the scroll

of Isaiah after having been to Jerusalem to worship. Look how the next verse begins:

> The Holy Spirit said to Philip . . .
> ACTS 8:29

While it's true that the Holy Spirit wants to communicate with us, let me offer one caution: don't wait for the Holy Spirit to speak out loud to you. Don't insist on a supernatural means of communication, because the God who gave us His Word expects you to go to His Word and hear Him there. He will speak to you through Scripture, with the Spirit's help. The Word of God will never fail to guide you if it's handled accurately and responsibly. In Philip's case, there wasn't a completed Bible yet, so the Holy Spirit intervened in a more direct way:

> The Holy Spirit said to Philip, "Go over and walk along beside the carriage."
> Philip ran over and heard the man reading from the prophet Isaiah. Philip asked, "Do you understand what you are reading?"
> The man replied, "How can I, unless someone instructs me?" And he urged Philip to come up into the carriage and sit with him.
> ACTS 8:29-31

Philip obeyed and ran over to the Ethiopian man. He said, in effect, "You are reading words, but do you understand what you're reading?" The man's response is wonderfully vulnerable: "How can I, unless someone instructs me?" What did the eunuch want? He wanted an interpreter. He was admitting, "I'm reading the words, but I don't know what they mean. I need you to help me—come sit with me."

Isn't that a great story? Philip saw this as a God-ordained opportunity. He climbed into the carriage and looked at the scroll where the man was reading:

The passage of Scripture he had been reading was this:

"He was led like a sheep to the slaughter.
   And as a lamb is silent before the shearers,
   he did not open his mouth.
He was humiliated and received no justice.
   Who can speak of his descendants?
   For his life was taken from the earth."

ACTS 8:32-33

When the eunuch was in Jerusalem, he had obtained a scroll of Isaiah, and on the way back he unrolled the scroll to Isaiah 53:7-8. He had probably never seen these words before. What in the world did they mean? Who was the "he" referred to in the prophecy? Notice the eunuch's question: "Tell me, was the prophet talking about himself or someone else?" (Acts 8:34).

Isn't that a great question? This man genuinely wanted to know the answer. Was Isaiah talking about himself in the third person—that he would be like a sheep led to slaughter? Or was he speaking of someone else? Philip, who knew the answer, must have thought, *Oh Lord, You are good. There I was in Samaria, not even knowing what was going on in Gaza, and You led me here to this carriage to sit beside this man. Now I have the privilege of telling him about You, the Lamb that was slaughtered.*

Philip knew that Isaiah 53 is a reference to the Messiah who would suffer and die. He explained it to the eunuch and later baptized him. The eunuch came full circle. When he started reading, he didn't know the Lord personally, but by the time he finished reading, the Lord had become his Savior. How? Because Philip carefully and correctly interpreted the Scripture for him.

Suppose I'm sitting in a Spanish-speaking church and the speaker is teaching in Spanish. I've gone there with a friend of mine who's bilingual, while I only know English. Imagine the speaker is saying something and the people laugh in response. Then he says something else, and the response is "Ooh"—clearly something profound was said. The rest of the audience is getting the message, while I'm sitting there with a blank look. Then my friend leans over and says, "Do you understand what you're hearing?"

"No, I can't understand," I reply. "I need an interpreter to explain what's being said."

My friend then translates the message, enabling me to understand.

GRASPING THE CONTEXT

Interpreting the Scriptures has to do with understanding what has been written. This might sound simple until you actually start digging into the Bible on your own. Observation is like excavation, which involves digging into the text to form the foundation of thought. Interpretation is the next step of the process, which involves the erection of the building. Once we've dug deeply and pushed the dirt aside, it's time for the next stage: determining what the text means. But suddenly we're faced with a couple of barriers. What are they?

1. **There's a language barrier.** The goal of interpretation is to understand what the original author meant. Keep in mind that the people who first recorded Scripture didn't write in English. The Old Testament Scriptures were

written primarily in Hebrew, and a few sections were written in Aramaic. However, most of us don't read Hebrew or Aramaic. Therefore, the Bible we use should be as accurate to the original text as possible. The version I prefer when I'm studying is the New American Standard Version. It's one of the more literal translations, and I appreciate its faithful rendering of the original languages. After I've finished studying and it's time for me to present a message, I prefer to use the New Living Translation, which is a reliable, easy-to-understand version.

For the New Testament, the original writing was in Greek. If Greek isn't your first language and if you haven't studied it, you will need a version of the Bible in your language that's as close to Greek as you can get. Again, I recommend the New American Standard Version for study and the New Living Translation for readability.

2. **There's a cultural barrier.** People in biblical times didn't live the same way we do today. The marriage customs in the first century weren't the same as ours in the twenty-first century. Children in Jesus' day weren't reared the way they are today. Some aspects of work were different in that era. A number of different cultural events have occurred in human history since the Bible was written. Therefore, to correctly interpret, we need to take into account the many cultural differences. This requires careful research.

Consider the words of scholar Bernard Ramm: "People of the same culture, same age, and same geographical location understand each other. . . . But when the interpreter is separated culturally, historically, and geographically from the writer . . . the task of interpretation is no longer facile. The greater the . . . divergences are, the more difficult is the task of interpretation." He continues, "The most obvious divergence is that of *language.* . . . There is also the *culture-gap* between our times and Biblical times."[8]

In the first century AD, Paul spoke of women needing to wear head coverings to church. They weren't to come for worship without it. If a woman were to read that today, she might think, *I need to go out and buy several hats for church. And I shouldn't cut my hair, because Paul writes about that, too.* Those are cultural issues we need to deal with when we interpret the Scriptures. It's easy to see how people have been led astray and become legalistic about certain aspects of Scripture because they didn't come to the correct conclusions in their cultural interpretations.

Ramm goes on to say, "Agricultural methods are different. Legal systems are different. Military systems are different. They're all very helpful in interpreting the Scriptures. And then there's geography. The understanding of most passages of Scripture is dependent on some understanding of history. If geography is the scenery of Scripture, history is the plot of Scripture."[9]

We need to become thoughtful students of the linguistic and cultural contexts in the Bible. Fortunately, there are many tools available to help us interpret the Bible. If you know where to look, there are many beneficial resources available online, and there are also useful software packages and apps. These tools can help you get serious about biblical interpretation. You don't have to go to seminary or learn another language, but you do need reliable tools and resources.

There are some crucial questions we need to ask when we're interpreting the Bible to ensure that we do it responsibly and accurately. A good place to start is by asking, "What is the setting?" Every verse has a context, even the first verse of the Bible. When we begin reading in the middle of a paragraph, as we did in Acts

8:26, we need to see what comes before and after the verse. We need to place the verses we're studying into their proper contexts. If we fail to do so, we will be awash, and it won't be long before we slide down the slippery slope of error. The context helps us hold true to the correct meaning.

SUGGESTED COMPUTER-BASED INTERPRETATION TOOLS

Logos Bible Software
This software is a digital library of research books, including commentaries, dictionaries, Bibles, and atlases.
www.logos.com

Olive Tree
This app can be used on a variety of digital devices and includes some free resources and some for purchase.
www.olivetree.com

Bible Study Tools
This free website offers many helpful resources for Bible study, including commentaries, concordances, and encyclopedias.
www.BibleStudyTools.com

PAY ATTENTION TO GENRES

Another important question to ask when we're interpreting Scripture is "What type of literature am I reading?" The story in Acts 8 is called a narrative. It recounts a larger story, connecting people and events and great ideas together. Each particular story is part of the overall narrative.

The Bible includes various genres, including *parables* in the New Testament. The term comes from the Greek word *parabole*, which is similar to our English word. *Parabole* means "to throw alongside." A parable throws one idea alongside another for the purpose of comparison. Mark 4 records a parable in which the farmer sows his seed on four different kinds of soil. We're not to take that literally, however. It's a parable, remember? But we have to be careful not to make any parable "walk on all fours." If we try to make every part of a parable perfectly symbolize or align with the realities of our world, we'll go mad. We're to draw truth from the parable as best we can, based on our overall knowledge of the Scriptures. In the case of Mark 4, Jesus interprets the parable for His disciples to describe what the four types of soils represent in everyday life.

This is a good time to mention a helpful saying I learned years ago: "If the normal sense makes good sense, seek no other sense." If you read a passage and it makes sense, don't look for some deeper meaning. You understand it. The story about the Prodigal Son (see Luke 15:11-32) is a parable. The account of the Good Samaritan (see Luke 10:30-37) is another parable. The one about the rich man (see Luke 12:16-21) is yet another. As we read these stories, it's important to remember that parables are a specific genre of Scripture. We need to tread softly and guard against stretching the meaning too far.

Another genre of the Scriptures that we need to interpret carefully is *poetry*. Hebrew poetry often contains a literary technique called parallelism, in which similar statements are repeated for emphasis and beauty.

> The LORD is my light and my salvation—
> so why should I be afraid?
> The LORD is my fortress, protecting me from danger,
> so why should I tremble?
>
> PSALM 27:1

Do these lines sound similar to each other? Of course, because they are parallel statements. The second line starts out the same as the first, and then it amplifies or explains the first line. When reading poetry, the heart must be engaged. There's emotion involved.

That's why the psalms include figurative language, colorful phrases, and beautiful literary devices. As you interpret biblical poetry, leave room for those features.

Consider the familiar words of Psalm 23. The chapter opens with these words:

> The LORD is my shepherd;
>   I have all that I need.

Now look at the parallelism:

> He lets me rest in green meadows;
>   he leads me beside peaceful
>   streams.
>   He renews my strength.
> He guides me along right paths,
>   bringing honor to his name.
>
> PSALM 23:2-3

All the verses following the opening line contain parallel thoughts, each of which offers a way of knowing that we will lack nothing since the Lord is our shepherd.

Another genre we need to be aware of is the *proverbial*. This style of writing is found in wisdom literature, which includes the book of Proverbs. Proverbs are filled with contrasts and comparisons. When we come to a contrasting word, we must remember that one word is often the direct opposite of another. Look at this example from the first chapter in Proverbs:

> Fear of the LORD is the foundation of true knowledge,
>   but fools despise wisdom and discipline.
>
> PROVERBS 1:7

The contrast is clear. There are those who fear the Lord, and they are contrasted with fools. It's critical for us to pay close attention to those opposite words as we interpret.

When we deal with *prophetic* literature in the Scriptures, we have to determine if the prophecy will be fulfilled in the ultimate future or if it was in the future when it was written but has already happened now.

Let's take a look at a prophetic passage in Isaiah 7:

All right then, the Lord himself will give you the sign. Look! The virgin will conceive a child! She will give birth to a son and will call him Immanuel (which means "God is with us").
ISAIAH 7:14

Isaiah wrote these words about seven hundred years before the birth of Christ. To Isaiah, this reference was to something that would happen in the future. Yet today we are living some two thousand years after the birth of Christ, so for us, this represents a completed prophecy. We are able to determine all this when we interpret prophetic literature.

COMMON TYPES OF BIBLICAL LITERATURE

Narrative: the events of Scripture
Parables: the stories of Jesus that teach a lesson
Poetry: the words of songs, such as the book of Psalms
Proverbial: the wisdom of Proverbs
Prophecy: the message of God given through His spokespeople

WATCH OUT FOR HAZARDS!

I must mention some of the more common hazards of interpretation. One of them is reading into the text what it doesn't say.

Watch out—this is a temptation all of us face. Here's one misinterpretation of Scripture you'll hear often: "If you have enough faith, God will heal you of every disease." The Bible doesn't teach that. That's been read into the text by those who want the Bible to say that. There are some definite guidelines about healing in the Scriptures, and if we ignore them, we'll be disillusioned when our suffering doesn't go away. Another mistake is thinking that a traditional saying comes from the Bible, like this false statement: "God helps those who help themselves." This phrase isn't found anywhere in the Scriptures. In fact, God says He helps the helpless (see Romans 5:6)!

Here's another: "God always blesses the faithful with material blessings." Not necessarily. While it's true that every good gift comes from the Lord (see James 1:17), God's blessings often come on the other side of eternity, not in the here and now. This ties in with another misinterpretation: "The more money you give to the Lord, the more He will give you in return." (There's a great Greek word for that: *hogwash*.) The prosperity gospel is built on materialistic promises. The Bible doesn't say if you give God money, then He'll give you more money in return. Otherwise, every generous person would be rich. That's not how it works. That's misinterpreting the text. In fact, Jesus commended a poor widow who gave everything she had without mentioning that she received anything in return (see Mark 12:42-44).

Another hazard to watch out for is oversight. When we read the Scriptures, we must guard against overlooking important words. For example, some people think 1 Timothy 6:10 says that "money is the root of all evil." The Bible doesn't teach that, however. The verse actually says, "*The love of* money is the root of all kinds of evil." If we overlook the first part of the verse, we'll twist the intended meaning. This happens when Scripture isn't read (and interpreted) correctly.

Here's another hazard of interpretation: becoming overly dogmatic and superconfident. It's amazing how often this happens when people begin to grow in their knowledge of the Bible. How much better to disarm others with our genuine humility. We can admit there's much we don't know and never will know. We need to stay teachable and remain gracious, regardless of our expanding knowledge of the Bible.

Theologian John R. W. Stott relates a humorous story about a young American Presbyterian minister whose besetting sin was conceit. He frequently boasted that all the time he needed to prepare his Sunday sermon was the few steps he took as he walked from the parsonage to the church next door. The elders, growing weary of his arrogance, bought a new home for their young minister—five miles away from the church.[10]

It doesn't matter how long you've been teaching the Scriptures—you are never the final authority. In fact, all of us are under the authority of the Word of God. This Book that speaks to everyone with its commands also speaks to the teacher or preacher. There is no place for arrogance. The knowledge of God can make us feel important, but as the New King James Version says, "Knowledge puffs up" (1 Corinthians 8:1). However, knowledge mixed with genuine understanding will keep us humble.

Years ago, someone passed along to me that "an education is best described as going from an unconscious to a conscious awareness of your ignorance." The more educated we become, the more we realize the vast amount of information we *don't* know. Every time I dig deeper into the Word of God, I realize how much I don't know. How thrilled I am to have some knowledge, but I realize that if I had ten lifetimes, I could never learn all there is to know from God's Book. As one of my seminary professors used to remind us in his classroom, "We have an infinite text. You'll never exhaust it."

FIVE ESSENTIAL QUESTIONS

Being a good chef requires many different skills: choosing a good recipe; selecting the right ingredients; shopping for each item (even a few exotic ones); organizing the kitchen; having the necessary tools, appliances, and utensils; and prepping the ingredients. A good chef does more than just throw the food into a pot and then turn up the heat. The same is true of Bible interpretation. Here are five essential questions every serious interpreter must ask herself or himself:

1. **Am I a believer in the Lord Jesus Christ?** God rarely illumines the minds of unbelievers with His truth. Scriptural insight is reserved for those who have the Spirit of God living in them. If you've never trusted in the Lord Jesus, this is a great moment for you to do so. Do you believe that He died for you on the cross and paid the full penalty for your sins? If you accept Him, you will have the assurance that your sins are forgiven and that you possess eternal life. Furthermore, when you trust in the Lord Jesus Christ, your inner life will be changed. Your eyes, once blind to the truths in God's Word, will be opened, and you will be able to see what you've never seen before.

2. **Do I have a passion to know God's Word?** The key word, of course, is *passion.* Is there an intense zeal within you, driving you to dig deeper? My study is on the second floor in our home. There are times I take those nineteen steps from our first floor up to the second floor two at a time; I can't wait to get up there! My passion to get into the Word of God is forever ablaze. I love the challenge of being able to study the Scriptures and then to deliver to others what the Lord has revealed to me. It's the most exciting part of my life—the fire

has never gone out. I freely confess that I am one motivated, excited chef!

3. **Have I humbled myself before the Lord?** Have you acknowledged your full dependence on Him, realizing that God and God alone must guide you into an understanding of His Word?

4. **Have I taken time to pray?** Study without prayer is an incomplete process—a futile effort. There's an old hymn with these words:

Speak, Lord, in the stillness,
While I wait on Thee;
Hushed my heart to listen,
In expectancy.

I often pray, "Lord, speak to me. Help me understand what this passage is saying. I am listening. I am sensitive to Your truth. Lead me into it. Don't let me misinterpret the message and drift into error."

5. **Have I done my homework well?** Have you dug deeply? Have you taken time to really think through the verse? Have you turned the words over in your mind? Have you asked penetrating questions? Have you searched this passage and others to be sure you've grasped the Lord's wisdom?

I've already stated that preparation for a delicious meal takes time. Beautiful feasts and celebratory meals don't happen quickly or haphazardly. The chefs involved in creating a gourmet meal have the skill and take the time to carefully plan and diligently prepare each course with precision and care.

The same is true of biblical interpretation. God doesn't reveal His truth to the hurried soul; you'll never go deep if you're in a rush. There's a process and an art to follow in interpreting well. Just as a chef knows the best utensils to use in meal preparation, a student of the Bible needs some key study tools, such as maps, concordances, Bible dictionaries, and commentaries, which will help with the task at hand. The most important tool of all is faith in Christ, which prompts us to rely on the Spirit to lead us into all truth (see 1 Corinthians 2:10-13).

The process doesn't stop here, though. Chefs don't spend all their time on just one dish. Flavors of various dishes must be compared so that each taste complements the other. It's the same with interpretation. We can't just look at one passage or an isolated verse. We need to understand the message across the entire story of Scripture, comparing with other relevant passages to ensure that we are understanding the text correctly. That's called correlation. In the next chapter, I'll show you how to do it correctly. Let the next course begin!

YOUR TURN IN THE KITCHEN

Cooking a nutritious and delicious meal requires an understanding of nutrients. The same is true when it comes to spiritual food: we need a careful understanding of the verses being
studied. Now it's time for you to develop your own skills and give
interpretation a try.

1. Read Romans 12:1-2:

> And so, dear brothers and sisters, I plead with you to give
> your bodies to God because of all he has done for you. Let
> them be a living and holy sacrifice—the kind he will find
> acceptable. This is truly the way to worship him. Don't
> copy the behavior and customs of this world, but let God
> transform you into a new person by changing the way
> you think. Then you will learn to know God's will for you,
> which is good and pleasing and perfect.

> Observe these words slowly and carefully so you begin to
> understand what they're saying. Take time to write down
> your observations.

Now let's work on coming to grips with what this passage

means. What does Paul mean when he writes, "Give your bodies to God"?

What is Paul referring to when he mentions "the behavior and customs of this world" (see Romans 1)?

What does it mean to "learn to know God's will for you"?

Take your time as you answer these questions. Tasty meals take time to prepare, and great chefs aren't in a hurry. Let the words simmer, and before long, the aroma will begin to emerge.

2. In the questions at the end of the previous chapter, you made observations on John 3:16 after reviewing all of John 3. Now it's time to see how the Bible helps to interpret itself. Often this is done when a New Testament passage interprets or explains an Old Testament passage. In John 3:14-15, Jesus refers to a story recorded in Numbers 21:4-9. Read this story of Moses lifting up the bronze snake on the pole and then make note of how it helps interpret what Jesus is saying to Nicodemus in John

3:14-15. If you're not sure, read the verses in both John and Numbers again. Again, take your time as you let the Scriptures soak in.

3. In the previous chapter, you made observations about Philippians 4:4-9; now it's time to interpret this passage. Review Philippians 1:1-30 to get some of the context in which Paul wrote this letter. In spite of Paul's imprisonment, what did he command the young church in the city of Philippi to do in Philippians 4:4-9? Why?

4. You've already made observations about Jesus' parable of the Good Samaritan. Now take some time to reread Luke 10:25-37 and explain Jesus' purpose in telling the parable. Why is this kind of storytelling a powerful way to teach? As you read these stories, remember that parables are a specific type of Scripture, so be sure to tread softly when studying them. Guard against stretching the meaning too far.

5. We have already made observations about the story of
   Daniel in the lions' den. Now let's return to Daniel 6:1-28
   and interpret the passage. What do we learn about God
   from this story? What do we learn about Daniel?

CHAPTER 6

COMPARING THE FLAVORS

Correlating the Text

COOKING IS BOTH A SCIENCE AND AN ART FORM. Steaks and pork chops respond to heat in different ways. The temperature of the grill must be calculated just right so the food isn't burned or underdone. A cut of meat cooked to scientific perfection is a culinary triumph and a delight to the senses. That said, great cooking is also an art. Knowing which special seasonings to use or just how much spice to add can make or break the meal. The skilled chef knows how to blend each ingredient to perfection, and the end result is delicious.

The same principle applies to studying the Word of God. We can get off track when we immerse ourselves in a single verse or an isolated passage of Scripture, unaware of other passages and references that can help us understand the subject more accurately. Much like chefs who cultivate the art of blending flavors, students of the Scriptures must carefully compare what they observe and interpret with other Bible passages so they don't misunderstand or misapply what they're reading.

There's a lot to consider when relating Old Testament commands with New Testament letters or when comparing Solomon's proverbs with Jesus' parables. Cultivating the art and science of correlating passages of the Bible will greatly enhance your knowledge of the Scriptures.

HOW TO HANDLE THE WORD OF GOD

If your childhood was like mine, the only Bible you were aware of was the King James Version—not the *New* King James, but the original 1611 edition. (I wasn't alive then, but I know it was published then.) I got used to the "thees," "thous," "therefores," "heretofores," and words like "charity" in place of "love" and "take heed" instead of "watch out." However, there were some passages that tripped me up. The verse about Jesus judging "the quick and the dead" (2 Timothy 4:1, KJV) always seemed strange to me. As a little boy, I remember thinking, *I understand "the dead," but those who are quick must be the ones trying to outrun Jesus when He comes after them.* It helped when I learned that this verse refers to the living and the dead. One passage I never quite got used to was Acts 17:5. The context is that a group of men hated what Paul was doing in the city of Thessalonica, so they got a bunch of wicked men together to stalk him. The King James Version describes them as "lewd fellows of the baser sort." Isn't that a quaint rendering? I'm not criticizing it; I'm just saying that it sounds unusual to our modern ears. There's another passage that baffled me, one that was always included in my list of Sunday school verses to memorize.

Study to shew thyself approved unto God, a workman that needeth not to be ashamed, rightly dividing the word of truth.

2 TIMOTHY 2:15, KJV

This sounded great, but I never knew what "rightly dividing" meant. No doubt this phrase was understood by those living in the seventeenth century, in the days of "King James English," but I ended up reciting words I didn't understand.

One teacher explained the verse this way: "You divide the Old Testament from the New Testament." But that has nothing to do with the meaning of that verse. Later I was taught that this verse referred to dividing the Bible into dispensations, or eras of time, from Genesis through Revelation. Again, that verse has little to do with dispensations. At a conference I attended as a young man, I heard a Bible teacher explain the verse this way: people who teach the Bible rightly divide the truth when they take it apart, divide it up, and then piece it back together. However, this isn't what 2 Timothy 2:15 is saying either.

The key word in this verse is *divide*, which comes from the Greek word *orthotomeo*. It's actually a combination of two Greek words. The first is *orthos* (where we get our words *orthodox* and *orthopedic*), which means "straight." *Temno* is a verb that means "to cut." It was used in the first century to refer to cutting a path through a forested area. The verse is essentially saying that we should cut a straight path to the truth as we allow it to speak clearly to us. That's what it means to "rightly divide." I love the way the New American Standard version renders this phrase: "accurately handling the word of truth." That's about as close as we can get to the original Greek.

If there were a single verse that summed up my calling, this would be it. My goal as an expositor is to accurately handle the Word of Truth. I will give an account to God for what I do with His Word. I have stood before congregations for more than fifty years, and when I open the Bible, I'm responsible for making sure I cut a straight path from the truth into life so that all who hear are led into an understanding of the truth.

WATCH OUT!

As you learn to handle God's Word, it's important to realize that there are unreliable and deceptive teachers who don't lead us to the truth. They take a portion of a verse and make it say something it was never meant to say, or they twist the entire meaning of a verse. They don't cut a straight path; they distort the truth, leading us to believe the Bible teaches something it doesn't.

In his book *Toxic Faith*, Stephen Arterburn shares this story about his grandmother:

> My grandmother died in 1989. If there were ever a person of strong faith and conviction, it was Nany. All alone she reared her three children, including my mother, after the suicide of my grandfather. She never gave up, never stopped believing, never lost faith. For her, death was merely a step into a better place. She didn't fear it. . . .
>
> At Nany's funeral, the minister told of one of the frustrations my grandmother had to endure: an audit by the Internal Revenue Service. The IRS went to a lot of trouble to make sure that someone who made every bit of eight thousand dollars a year paid her fair share of income taxes. While others were hiding millions of dollars from the federal government, special agents were hard at work on the case of Pearl Russell, making sure the country would not be shorted a few hundred dollars by a sweet old lady in Athens, Texas.
>
> At issue was Nany's large deduction for charitable contributions. The government could not believe that a woman making so little could give 35, and some years 40, percent to the church and still have enough money left over to pay her bills. The IRS finally backed off when she dug out of the attic all the canceled checks to television ministers, radio preachers, and her local church. Agents did not

understand it, but they were convinced that she had given every penny she had deducted. . . .

There was nothing toxic about Nany's faith. She never gave to a particular minister, but always to the ministry, such as to a children's home or to a project to feed the homeless. When she gave a dollar, she knew how that minister was going to spend it.

At least she thought she did.

Some of the individuals to whom she gave her money were not so admirable. Their toxic faith robbed my grandmother of the great blessing of knowing her money had been used to further the kingdom of God. They took her money and spent it on themselves and their big plans, schemes that had nothing to do with my grandmother's desire to tell the world about God's love or to feed and clothe orphans. Some of those ministers that she so faithfully supported wound up in jail, divorced their wives, or were arrested for indecent exposure, or fell into other public sin. They proclaimed a faith on television or over the radio, but they lived something else. They didn't shrink from asking my grandmother and others like her to sacrifice their food money so they could buy jet fuel to fly to Palm Springs for a weekend getaway. What they did was dishonest, unfair—and very human. The kind of faith they lived looked radically different from the one they proclaimed on the public airwaves.

These unfaithful men and women who spent Nany's money put more faith in themselves than they did in God. They relied more on their manipulations than on God's providence. . . . Their faith was toxic. It poisoned many who trusted them, and it distorted the view of God held by many who watched as these media ministers fell from grace. . . .

These cynics have derived a toxic, unhealthy view of faith from the toxic examples they saw in the media.[11]

How tragic! Those greedy false teachers distorted the Word of God, and sadly, they aren't the only ones. Some preachers and teachers twist the meaning of Scripture to manipulate their naive followers.

Just a few weeks ago, I heard a false teacher stand in front of a television audience and say, "Our worship isn't about God; it's about *us*. God wants us to be happy. We come together to be happy. This isn't about God; it's about *us*!" That bald-faced lie is based on a twisted view of Scripture. If you don't know how to accurately handle the Word of God, it's easy to be taken in by teaching that wraps itself around the name of religion.

We gain discernment when we make a serious study of the Scriptures. We become mature as we grow in the knowledge of what God has actually said. We cut that straight line toward our destination: exactly what God says, which is exactly what God means. God's Word has been supernaturally revealed and preserved for us so that we might accurately examine and understand it. As we will see, one of the most important ways to accomplish that goal is by comparing Scripture with Scripture. By doing so, we are less likely to drift into error.

WHAT IS CORRELATION?

The first part of Bible study we covered was observation. Next we considered interpretation. Both are essential in coming to an understanding of the Bible. But there's another part of the process: *correlation*. By comparing one Scripture with other Scriptures, precept upon precept and line upon line, the whole truth begins to emerge. Correlation amplifies our understanding of what the Bible is teaching. For example, Matthew 6:5-7 talks about prayer, but the Bible says something else about prayer in James 4:3 and Psalm 66:18. The Bible includes even more on prayer in Philippians 4:6-7.

CORRELATION

Comparing one Scripture with other Scriptures, precept upon precept and line upon line, to amplify our understanding of what the Bible is teaching

---

The most reliable students of the Bible are those who take the time to compare one Scripture with others. This discipline guards us from falling into error as we seek to gain a more thorough understanding of the truth.

The late Donald Grey Barnhouse, one of the great Bible teachers of yesteryear, underscored the importance of correlation: "You very rarely have to go outside of the Bible to explain anything in the Bible."[12] This is true because the Bible is the only perfectly correlated book on earth. There are no contradictions. Though cynics will try to convince us otherwise, the inerrancy of Scripture assures us that we can trust God's Word. This explains why the trustworthiness of the Bible is debated from one generation to the next. It will always be *the* crucial issue. Take away the inerrancy of Scripture, and we're adrift. Thankfully, God's Word remains solid and sure.

What we have in the Scriptures is sixty-six individual parts of one perfectly coordinated book, written by forty human writers with one divine Author, the Holy Spirit, who has watched over the preservation and integration of the text. I've studied the Scriptures for well over fifty years, and I have yet to find any contradiction or misinformation in this Book. There isn't a hint of erroneous advice, not one unimportant warning. It's filled with only reliable truth. Our task as students of the Bible is to cut a straight path to it, not twist it or stray from it.

For the next few moments, let's correlate what we just read in 2 Timothy 2:15 with Paul's first letter to Timothy. In 1 Timothy 1:5, Paul states his purpose as a teacher of the truth:

> The purpose of my instruction is that all believers would be filled with love that comes from a pure heart, a clear conscience, and genuine faith.

Paul begins by clearly and specifically stating his purpose. This verse means exactly what it says. Paul wanted people to be filled with love from pure hearts, to have a clear conscience and genuine faith. How magnificent! The next verse declares:

> But some people have missed this whole point. They have turned away from these things and spend their time in meaningless discussions.
> 1 TIMOTHY 1:6

Take note of how Paul begins: "But." Remember what we learned regarding the value of observation? Every word is important. *But* is a word of contrast. It introduces an idea that stands in contrast to what Paul has just written. Having stated the purpose of instruction, he mentions others who "have turned away from these things." What things? The things Paul just mentioned: a pure heart, a clear conscience, and genuine faith. Then Paul offers this further indictment:

> They . . . spend their time in meaningless discussions. They want to be known as teachers of the law of Moses, but they don't know what they are talking about, even though they speak so confidently.
> 1 TIMOTHY 1:6-7

Paul doesn't hold back when he describes erroneous teachers. They look like they know what they're talking about, but when you probe the truth on your own, you realize that if you'd believed what they taught, you would have been led astray. The fallout is dreadful, just as it was for the grandson of the generous woman we read about earlier in this chapter, who never realized her financial donations were supporting false teaching.

Correlating Scripture is invaluable. When we carefully compare one Scripture with others, we are accurately handling the Word of God.

TOOLS TO HELP IN CORRELATION

Here are five tools that will help you as you learn to correlate verses (note that a number of these resources were mentioned in chapter 3):

1. **A good study Bible.** Choose the Bible and the version you wish. One option I recommend is the *Ryrie Study Bible* in the New American Standard version, which does a trustworthy job providing the reader with reliable information. You may also consider the *New Living Translation Study Bible*, which is succinct and easy to understand. Whatever Bible you select, be sure it provides sufficient space to write notes in the margin and offers helpful comments at the bottom of the page.

2. **A concordance.** This tool is like an index to the Bible, as it features an alphabetical listing of all the words in Scripture. Without a concordance, you're left to flip haphazardly from one verse to another. It's important to make sure your concordance corresponds to the version of the Bible you're using so that the words match. For example, if you look up the word *love* in a concordance but your translation uses the

word *charity*, you may not find the results you're looking for. If you're using the New International Version, you'll need an NIV concordance. If you're using the King James, you need *Young's Concordance* or *Strong's Concordance*. There are many digital versions as well. Logos Bible Software is available for purchase and contains a digital library of Bibles and research books. You can search any word in any of the Bible versions included in the software. The Olive Tree app can be purchased for various phones and tablets. It allows you to search for any word in any version of the Bible available on the app. There are also websites such as www.BibleStudyTools.com and www.BibleGateway.com that allow you to search for words and phrases for free. All these tools are valuable for Bible study.

3. **A Bible dictionary.** This is a helpful tool for explaining background material and Bible history. Without it, you will have an incomplete understanding of what you're studying. Two reliable sources are *Unger's Bible Dictionary* and the *Zondervan Bible Dictionary*. You can also ask a clerk at a Christian bookstore for recommendations, or you can use online sources such as www.BibleStudyTools.com and www.BibleGateway.com.

4. **A one-volume Bible handbook.** A handbook gives you a simple, concise encyclopedia of the Scriptures. It provides brief summaries, helping you to cover many bases in a short time. Many reliable handbooks are available, but the one I use is *Halley's Bible Handbook*.

5. **Commentaries.** I always use commentaries when I prepare, but I don't turn to them until after I've done my own study

in the Scriptures. Commentaries from qualified authors provide helpful insights you might not catch on your own.

These tools are like a chef's essential utensils in the kitchen. Without them, preparing the meal takes much more time and effort, and the results may not be as rewarding.

CORRELATING PASSAGES ON KEEPING THE FAITH

Let's look at another example of correlation, this time from the writings of the apostle Peter. He wanted his readers to keep growing strong in the faith even after he died, so he wrote them this message:

> Therefore, I will always remind you about these things—
> even though you already know them and are standing firm
> in the truth you have been taught.
>
> 2 PETER 1:12

Peter faithfully taught God's truth. He went straight to the scrolls of the Old Testament and drew information from them. In doing so, he led his readers into the truth.

> And it is only right that I should keep on reminding you as
> long as I live. For our Lord Jesus Christ has shown me that I
> must soon leave this earthly life, so I will work hard to make
> sure you always remember these things after I am gone.
>
> 2 PETER 1:13-15

A little later in the same chapter, Peter mentions the prophets:

> Above all, you must realize that no prophecy in Scripture
> ever came from the prophet's own understanding.
>
> 2 PETER 1:20

The King James Version translates the verse this way: "No prophecy of the scripture is of any private interpretation." In other words, the prophet didn't originate his message and then write it down; God gave it to him. It wasn't derived from his own initiative; God supernaturally revealed the information. And Peter, as one of the inspired writers of Scripture, was chosen by God to be one of those original writers. The end of that verse explains the Lord's role in communicating truth to His people:

> No, those prophets were moved by the Holy Spirit, and they spoke from God.
>
> 2 PETER 1:21

Peter was writing about the Old Testament prophets. He correlated what the prophets said in previous generations and applied it to his own writing.

Let's examine the phrase "moved by the Holy Spirit." The word *moved* is the interesting Greek word *pheró* (pronounced like pharaoh, the title for an ancient Egyptian leader). *Pheró* means "to bear, carry, or bring." (By the way, I found that definition in my Bible dictionary.) This is a nautical term used to describe a ship or a boat that has lost its rudder and sails. As a result, it's at the mercy of the sea, with the wind and the waves moving the vessel outside its own power. The ancient prophets who spoke and wrote God's truth did so apart from their own abilities—the Holy Spirit led and empowered them. Look at the verse again. Let's "cut a straight path."

> Above all, you must realize that no prophecy in Scripture ever came from the prophet's own understanding, or from human initiative. No, those prophets were moved by the Holy Spirit, and they spoke from God.
>
> 2 PETER 1:20-21

The prophets were supernaturally *moved* or *directed* by God to record His messages. We have the right to interpret Scripture, but we don't have the right to distort it. Scripture represents the original, actual words of God, so we dare not twist its meaning!

In the Dark Ages, the clergy insisted that the common man or woman couldn't understand what Scripture taught. The Bible version that was used at the time was in Latin, a language that only the highly educated could read. The Bible was often chained to a pulpit, to be read only by priests. During the Protestant Reformation, the biblical truth spread that Jesus Himself intercedes for us before the Father. We don't need to rely on a human priest to understand God's truth; we're qualified to pursue it on our own. This is verified for us in Hebrews 4:

> So then, since we have a great High Priest who has entered heaven, Jesus the Son of God, let us hold firmly to what we believe. This High Priest of ours understands our weaknesses, for he faced all of the same testings we do, yet he did not sin. So let us come boldly to the throne of our gracious God. There we will receive his mercy, and we will find grace to help us when we need it most.
>
> HEBREWS 4:14-16

Thanks to these three verses in Hebrews 4, we discover that Jesus represents us before God. We don't pray through a pastor or a priest. Now that Christ has come and fulfilled the law, we can go directly to God. We don't need to rely on a religious leader to find out what the Bible is teaching either. We can read and understand the Book of God ourselves. This means we're free from relying on any human being for biblical intake. We can compare Scripture with Scripture on our own and thereby be led to the truth. We can cut that straight path into an understanding of God's truth.

Now let's turn to 2 Peter 3 and correlate these Scriptures.

And remember, our Lord's patience gives people time to be saved. This is what our beloved brother Paul also wrote to you with the wisdom God gave him.

2 PETER 3:15

Do you realize how remarkable this is? Peter is referring to another writer of Scripture, Paul. Notice what he says:

This is what our beloved brother Paul also wrote to you with the wisdom God gave him—speaking of these things in all of his letters. Some of his comments are hard to understand, and those who are ignorant and unstable have twisted his letters to mean something quite different, just as they do with other parts of Scripture. And this will result in their destruction.

2 PETER 3:15-16

There is comfort in Peter's honesty. Paul's writings were hard for Peter to understand, just as they are hard for us to understand at times. We're in good company! Peter says, essentially, "I read some of the things Paul wrote, and it's hard for me to understand them."

Notice what Peter is saying about Paul's writing: people have twisted his words. This word "to twist" is the Greek word *strebloo*. In his outstanding lexicon, Walter Bauer says this word means "to distort a statement so that a false meaning results."[13] In a commentary on 2 Peter, William Barclay says, "Paul's doctrine of *grace* was twisted into an excuse and reason for sin (Romans 6). Paul's doctrine of Christian *freedom* was twisted into an excuse for un-Christian licence (Galatians 5:13). Paul's doctrine of *faith* was twisted into an argument that Christian action was unimportant, as we see in James (James 2:14-26)."[14] In other words, people misconstrued Paul's words to make them easier to swallow.

I've been told that my teaching on grace will lead people into sin. Some think I'm guilty of twisting the meaning of grace as revealed in the Scriptures. Actually, I've remained true to God's Word, but some people are afraid of grace because it gives all believers the freedom to make choices. Unfortunately, some people do go too far, and as a result, they suffer the consequences of living in license. There are people who twist Paul's writings to say the same thing. However, that's not what he's saying. It can be easy to slip into heresy if we're not careful; we need to be vigilant about guarding the truth.

Barclay also tells us, "G. K. Chesterton once said that orthodoxy was like walking along a narrow ridge; one step to either side was a step to disaster. Jesus is God and man; God is love and holiness; Christianity is grace and morality; Christians live in this world and in the world of eternity. Overemphasize either side of these great two-sided truths, and immediately destructive heresy emerges."[15]

It's writing like this that prompts me to pray, "Lord, keep me balanced. Let me not be afraid of preaching grace; just help me to preach it correctly so people know they're free from the legalistic demands of others but don't assume they're free to do whatever they want to do." We need the kind of liberty that releases us from legalism and guides us into obedience to Christ and the marvelous truths set forth in the Scriptures (see Galatians 5:13).

CORRELATING PASSAGES ON PRAYER

To show you how correlation works from start to finish, let's go through the process together on the topic of prayer. First, look at what Jesus taught his disciples about the topic:

Then Jesus told them, "I tell you the truth, if you have
faith and don't doubt, you can do things like this and
much more. You can even say to this mountain, 'May you
be lifted up and thrown into the sea,' and it will happen.
You can pray for anything, and if you have faith, you will
receive it."

MATTHEW 21:21-22

Wow! We'd love it if all the teaching on prayer would stop there, as
if prayer simply involved asking God for something and then getting exactly what we asked for. But that's not all the Bible has to
say on the topic. We're cautioned in 1 John 5 to ask for whatever
pleases God, not ourselves.

And we are confident that he hears us whenever we ask for
anything that pleases him. And since we know he hears us
when we make our requests, we also know that he will give
us what we ask for.

1 JOHN 5:14-15

James adds more. He writes that we're supposed to pray with clear,
clean motives:

And even when you ask, you don't get it because your
motives are all wrong—you want only what will give you
pleasure.

JAMES 4:3

In other words, we need to examine our motives.

Psalm 66:18 offers this warning about praying when we have
unconfessed sin in our lives:

If I had not confessed the sin in my heart,
the Lord would not have listened.

We need to correlate Jesus' words in Matthew 21 with John's instruction in 1 John 5 . . . and also with James's warning and the psalmist's counsel. That is what keeps us from making false statements based on single-verse interpretations. Correlation shows that "name it and claim it" teaching is incorrect and therefore unreliable. God's Word correlated with God's Word keeps us on the straight and narrow path of correct thinking and righteous living.

BEWARE OF OBSCURITY

Be careful about building a doctrine based on one verse—especially an obscure verse. For example, when King Saul reached the end of his life, he was depressed and didn't know where to turn, so he visited a witch (see 1 Samuel 28). The witch of Endor conjured a person from the dead through the power of the devil. When you read about that, you might think, *Wow, look at that.* But beware of building your whole doctrine of devil and demons on an obscure section of Scripture. Correlation urges us to look elsewhere when forming our doctrinal foundations regarding Satan and his sinister forces, demons.

When the movie *The Exorcist* was released, all kinds of weird information began to circulate about Satan and demons. People were afraid there were demons lurking in every corner after watching the film. I decided to learn about this topic firsthand, so I did a thorough study of demons and the devil in Scripture. Do you know what happened after I did that study? I lost all fear of the devil, because I learned that his power is limited. Knowing what Scripture actually says helped me combat all the confusing comments that were being tossed around about the devil and demons. What saved me from confusion? Correlation.

DEMON CONTACT IN THE NEW TESTAMENT

	Luke 4:40-41	Mark 5:1-15	Mark 9:14-29
Victim	many who were sick	a man	a man's son
Tormentor	demons	demons; evil spirits; "Legion"	evil spirit
Victim's Experience	possessed by a demon	lived near tombs; possessed super-human strength; suicidal	mute; suicidal; suffering from seizures since childhood
Method to Expel Demons	Jesus laid hands on victims, and He cast out and rebuked the demons.	Jesus asked the demons their name ("Legion"). He cast them out of the man and granted their request to be sent into a herd of pigs.	Jesus rebuked the evil spirit and healed the boy.
Demon's Response	The demons cried out, "You are the Son of God!"	They knew Jesus was the Son of God. They asked Him to send them into the pigs, which then drowned.	It screamed, threw the boy into a violent convulsion, and left.
Final Result	healing	complete relief; in his right mind	healing

How did I do this study on demons? I simply opened my Bible, and with the help of my concordance, I checked every reference to demons in the New Testament. In each passage, I observed who the victim was and who the tormentor was. I noted the victim's experience and the method Jesus used to expel demons. I wrote down the demon's response and the final result. You don't have to be a Bible scholar to do that, but you do need to study and think . . . and then let Scripture speak for itself. I'm so grateful I did that study! In doing so, I armed myself against superstition and false information.

WHY CORRELATION IS VITAL

There are at least four major benefits to correlating Scripture with Scripture:

1. **Correlation gives us clear discernment instead of vague opinions.** Human opinions are a dime a dozen—and most of them are wrong. Correlation moves the authority from us to Scripture itself.

2. **As our knowledge of Scripture broadens, our understanding of God will deepen.** This gives us great biblical stability.

3. **Correlation helps us cultivate a reasonable and balanced faith.** It protects from extremes. Satan is the expert of extremes, whereas Scripture provides the bulwark of balance.

4. **Correlation enables us to separate truth from error quickly.** When we're confronted with false teaching, whether at our front door or in the pulpit at church, we'll be able to recognize it and confront it with Scripture.

Now that we've looked at some of the benefits of correlation, let me close this chapter by pointing out a few essentials for correlation:

> **Be diligent.** Dig in! Don't rely on my teaching; you
> need to do your own study. Even if you have only thirty
> minutes a day, shut off the TV and sit quietly before the
> Lord with your Bible open. Be conscientious as you fulfill
> your task as a careful student of the Scriptures.

> **Please God.** You're not looking to please anyone else;
> you're becoming strong in the Scriptures. Most of us have
> friends whose faith is distorted. It's not your job to help
> them feel good about themselves or to like you more—you
> don't need their approval. You want to be approved by
> God. Remember 2 Timothy 2:15: "Work hard so you can
> present yourself to God and receive his approval." Careful
> study in the Word of God honors the God of the Word.
> He smiles on every moment you spend in the Scriptures.
> As you study, remember to pray, asking God to guide you.

> **Stay balanced.** Don't wander or go to extremes. If you
> sense that a discovery in Scripture is out of balance,
> it probably is. Keep focused on God's Word, and seek
> truth. Cut a straight path for it.

As I've mentioned before, working in the kitchen is a learned skill.
Comparing the flavors doesn't come naturally to most people. We
learn how ingredients taste and in what proportion to use them. We
cultivate the necessary skills and collect the right utensils to prepare
the food. We learn to present a meal that is attractive, delicious, and
nutritious. All that takes time. It also requires taking the right steps
in the right order. All the while, we're looking for great taste and
good nutritional value. It's even more important to find the right
taste and nutritional value in the spiritual food we digest. In fact,
Psalm 34:8 tells us to "taste and see that the LORD is good."

After carefully observing a piece of Scripture and interpreting its meaning, we correlate what we've read with other passages. This is our safety valve. It helps us to know if we've interpreted the passage correctly. It saves us from those who are careless and manipulative with the sacred text. This is a mandatory step that leads to the crowning achievement of Bible study: application. We must present the Scriptures in a way that's compelling for us and others. In the next chapter, we'll walk into that all-important world of practical application.

Learning to compare the flavors in cooking takes time, and it's often accomplished through a lot of experimentation. Correlating the Scriptures works the same way; you won't learn how to do it until you actually give it a try. Here are a few exercises to help you begin.

1. Using my chart on page 152 as an example, fill in the chart below by looking up the passages and recording the details.

DEMON CONTACT IN THE NEW TESTAMENT

	Mark 3:10-11	Luke 4:31-35	Acts 16:16-18
Victim			
Tormentor			
Victim's Experience			
Method to Expel Demons			
Demon's Response			
Final Result			

2. What can you learn by correlating these three accounts of demon contact in the New Testament?

3. What consistencies do you see when you look at each of the following categories: the victim's experience, the demon's response, and the final result?

4. In our study of John 3, we saw that Jesus told Nicodemus that the Son of Man must be lifted up. Several times in the book of John, Jesus makes similar statements. Read John 8:27-28 and John 12:31-36. How do these two passages help us understand Jesus' statement to Nicodemus in John 3?

5. We have already begun our study of Philippians 4:4-9, in which Paul addresses the importance of prayer. Now it's time to correlate Paul's teaching with other key passages that will help us understand what Paul means. Carefully read Matthew 6:5-7, James 4:3, and Psalm 66:18, and observe what they say. How do these passages help us gain a broader understanding of Paul's statement on prayer in Philippians 4:4-9?

6. In Luke 10:25-37, Jesus tells the story of the Good Samaritan in response to a question about loving one's neighbor. Read Leviticus 19:15-18, Romans 13:8-10, and Galatians 5:14. How do these verses help us to understand the importance of the parable about the Good Samaritan?

CHAPTER 7

ADDING THE SPICES

Applying the Text

Each step that goes into making a gourmet meal contributes to an exciting culinary experience. This includes shopping for the best ingredients, cleaning and cutting the vegetables, grilling the meat to perfection, and finally presenting the meal on fine china with exquisite crystal. Of course, what makes or breaks the meal is how the first bite tastes to the palate. All the diligent preparation and careful presentation fades compared to how the food actually tastes.

The same can be said for studying and digesting the Scriptures. Up until this chapter, we've given our attention to careful observation, accurate interpretation, and comprehensive correlation. However, all of that is incomplete without personal and insightful application. Failing to apply the Scriptures would be like creating a delicious meal but never actually sitting down and tasting it for yourself.

In 1959, as a first-year seminary student, I sat on the edge of my seat during Bible Study Methods. Dr. Hendricks began the class with a shocking statement: "If you observe and interpret and correlate the Scriptures but fail to apply the Scriptures, you have committed an abortion." The vivid word picture made me realize what a tragedy it is to do the hard work of studying the sacred Scriptures and coming to an understanding of what they say and mean, only to fail to apply them personally. Without application, you have thwarted new life. For it is in the application of the truth that we find conviction, direction, correction, and encouragement for our spiritual growth. Application is the crowning accomplishment of Bible study—the finishing touch, the ultimate setting of the diamond in the ring of truth.

I've never forgotten those penetrating words from Dr. Hendricks. They still haunt me. Every time I sit down to prepare a message, I remember his admonition and other teachings like it: "Study hard. Read thoroughly and carefully so you observe what the Bible is saying. Spend time in interpretation so the Spirit of God can lead you to an understanding of the meaning of this passage, initially in the mind of the writer himself and ultimately in the lives of those who live centuries after the text was written."

I repeat: the crowning part of your task in searching the Scriptures is to discover ways the truth applies to your own life and the lives of others. If we fail to apply what we've studied, we deprive ourselves of the magnificent truth of the Word, which is meant to nourish us. If you are a teacher of an adult fellowship or a Sunday school class or a small group, make certain you not only teach what the various verses say and mean but also take the time to spell out how those same verses touch the nerve center of some specific facet of life. The satisfaction that comes from doing so is too wonderful for words, much like the feeling that comes after sharing a sumptuous meal with those we love.

James reminds us, "Remember, it is sin to know what you ought to do and then not do it" (James 4:17). I urge you to take that admonition personally. It is incomplete to explain what the Lord has written in His Word and then walk away with mere knowledge, with no plans to follow through with obedience.

Cynthia and I sat under the teaching of a very fine preacher and Bible scholar for a number of years. He could explain the text masterfully. He could analyze the verses as well as anyone I had ever heard. His theology was impeccable. He had incredible insight into the Scriptures. But toward the end of his message, he would usually say, "May the Lord apply these verses to our lives." This statement would be followed by, "And now let's pray." I often thought, *No! You need to help us apply these verses! You're the one who helped us understand what they say and what they mean. Help us discover their significance in our lives. Spell it out—get specific!* We as the congregation were usually left to do that on our own. It was like getting up from a meal and still feeling hungry. His exposition was insightful but incomplete.

WHAT IS APPLICATION?

What do we mean when we talk about applying the Bible to our lives? Application means that we take God's Word personally. It means we see how it addresses specific areas of our everyday lives. It's allowing the Bible's truths to grip us in areas that need attention and to call us to action. If I present the gospel of the Lord Jesus Christ to you and tell you that Jesus Christ died for your sins according to the Scriptures; if I explain that He was buried and shortly thereafter was miraculously raised from the grave; and if I tell you that Christ's death and resurrection paid the complete penalty for your sin, giving you the opportunity to have eternal life; but I stop there, all you have is a set of facts. Yes, they're true and reliable, but the message is incomplete. If, however, I say, "You must receive this message personally," you are left to respond—to apply the entire message of the gospel. You are free to accept that message or reject it, to believe it or refuse it. To use fishing terms, I set the hook. To use fund-raising terms, I do the ask. To use football terms, I throw the pass. To use culinary terms, I serve the meal.

APPLICATION

Allowing the truths of God's Word to grip us in areas that need attention and to call us to action

---

Lewis Sperry Chafer, the founder of Dallas Theological Seminary, used to say, "You have not preached the gospel until you have given people something to believe." You believe in the Lord Jesus Christ when you trust Him, when you rely on Him to forgive your sins and give you eternal life. You have, by faith, taken into your life the person of Christ. From that moment on, the Holy Spirit resides within you. Furthermore, you are declared righteous before God. At that point, you are given specific spiritual gifts that are to be used in the body of Christ. However, none of this transpires if you fail to apply the gospel personally. Remember, it is sin to know what we should do and then not do it. In the simplest of terms, application is *obedience in action*.

WHY IS APPLICATION IMPORTANT?

There are at least three reasons why personal application is important:

1. **We need to practice what we say we believe.** The book of James revolves around this theme. In effect, those five chapters are saying that if we say we believe, why would we behave as if we didn't? That's why James invites us to come to the mirror of the Word of God and to see the true

condition of our inner lives. Once we see what's there, we take the necessary steps to deal with the behaviors and attitudes that need to change. Why? Because we need to apply what we believe.

2. **Both the Old and the New Testament exhort us to do so.** (See, for example, Deuteronomy 11:1 and James 1:22.) We need to apply the commands of Scripture so we become obedient followers of Christ. We're not to be blind, passive followers; we're to be obedient, active followers. We take in the truth, and then we obey it. Remember, God did not give us His Word to satisfy our curiosity; He gave it to us to transform our lives.

3. **Application enables us to operate our lives in the power of the Holy Spirit.** As I apply the truth, the Spirit of God is supernaturally at work within me. Before Christ left this earth, He commissioned His disciples to go into all the world and spread His truth. He said, in effect, "You carry on until I come back" (see Luke 19:11-27). He expected His followers to put His instructions into practice.

Let's imagine that I'm the CEO of a large corporation, and you are an employee of this company. My responsibility includes travel, and at one point I'm scheduled to make a lengthy tour of other countries. I tell you that while I'm gone, I expect you to faithfully carry on with your work. Before I leave, I gather together all the employees who are part of the corporation and say, "Look, while I'm gone, I'm going to send you at least one e-mail every week that explains what I want done while I'm away. I don't need to be here because you're able to follow these instructions." Everybody understands and agrees.

While I'm gone, I faithfully write a weekly e-mail to you and the rest of the company stating what I expect and what you are to do in my absence. I make it clear; there is no confusion. Time passes, and each week you receive my instructions. Finally, my trip comes to an end.

When I return, I drive up to the building and immediately notice that grass is growing in the cracks of the parking lot. A lot of trash is blowing around on the grounds. I walk in the front door and the receptionist is leaning back in her chair doing her nails, watching a show on her laptop. Some employees who are into fantasy football are betting on football games, talking about which team won last weekend and which team is likely to win this weekend. I look back toward your office and notice that you and several other employees are playing video games. You're laughing it up and having a great time.

"Hold it," I say. "What's going on here?"

"Oh, welcome back!" you reply. "It's great to have you back."

"Didn't you get my e-mails?"

"Yes, we did," one employee responds. "In fact, we got every single one. You're a great writer! We were fascinated by the messages you sent. In fact, we had various people meet in small groups to study your e-mails. We were especially interested in your words regarding the future, because we get excited thinking about future things. In fact, we have a group that has memorized some of the most well-written lines from your e-mails. We really enjoyed what you sent us."

I stare at the group, shaking my head. Then I say, "I have a question to ask all of you. What did you *do* about the things I wrote?"

Suddenly everyone gets a blank look on their faces.

"Do?" you ask. "We didn't *do* anything about them, but we were faithful to read and study them and even memorize some of them."

"That doesn't matter! I sent you those messages so you would carry out the instructions in my absence."

What was missing? *Application.*

This illustrates how we as followers of Christ often treat the Scriptures God has given us. If we overlook application—if we simply make a study of what He wrote but don't follow through on the responsibilities He has assigned us—the consequences will be tragic.

WHEN APPLICATION IS OVERLOOKED

Let's look at what happens to us spiritually when we don't apply the Scriptures:

1. **Doctrine becomes dusty, dry, and lifeless.** We could fill our heads and our notebooks with information about the doctrines of God, Christ, the Holy Spirit, Satan, demons, angels, sin, salvation, and the church. Then we could study the truths regarding future things. We could even add forgiveness, grace, the Cross, and all that goes with these great truths. But without application, none of those subjects make any difference in how we live. The doctrine may bounce around in our heads for a while, but it falls flat when our lives don't change for the better.

2. **We substitute rationalization for repentance.** If we don't apply God's Word, we hear what the Scriptures are saying, but we aren't convicted. We don't realize that these words are for us to live out, not simply to study, memorize, and talk about.

3. **We think emotional experiences replace a volitional decision.** We may feel guilty over some recurring sin or feel sad over our impatience and anger, but that's merely the first

step toward application. When we feel the conviction of the Spirit of God at work within us, it gives us the tools to apply it in specific ways, whether that means making tough decisions, addressing specific addictions, or confessing long-standing sins.

THE PROCESS OF SELF-EXAMINATION

Responding to the conviction of the Holy Spirit is the initial part of application. This process is sometimes called self-examination. At the end of 1 Corinthians 11, we read an exhortation about observing the Lord's Table. Eating the bread and drinking from the cup remind us of what each represents: the body and blood of our Lord Jesus. But we're not to just waltz into a church service, sit down, have a little piece of bread, drink a small cup of juice, and then skate out the exit. No, we're responsible for preparing ourselves spiritually. Just as we wash our hands before eating a meal, we bring our lives before the Lord and ask Him to clean our hearts before we come to the Table. That's what this passage is teaching. Think deeply as you read what the apostle Paul wrote:

> For every time you eat this bread and drink this cup, you are announcing the Lord's death until he comes again.
>
> So anyone who eats this bread or drinks this cup of the Lord unworthily is guilty of sinning against the body and blood of the Lord. That is why you should examine yourself before eating the bread and drinking the cup.
>
> I CORINTHIANS 11:26-28

Maybe you never thought of it this way, but the Lord's Table is a public announcement of the Savior's death on our behalf. Notice Paul's direct command to "examine" ourselves. The Greek term is *dokimazo*, which means "to make a critical examination of something to determine its genuineness." When I examine myself before eating the bread and drinking the cup, I look at any part of my life that's hypocritical, not genuine. I ask myself if I'm guilty of a cover-up. In which parts of my life—my mind, my thoughts, my motives, my words, or my actions—does my self-examination reveal a lack of genuineness?

Through correlation we learn that the same word appears in 2 Corinthians 13:5, where Paul states, "*Examine* yourselves to see if your faith is genuine. Test yourselves. Surely you know that Jesus Christ is among you; if not, you have failed the test of genuine faith" (emphasis added).

Let's continue with the apostle's instructions in 1 Corinthians 11:

> For if you eat the bread or drink the cup without honoring the body of Christ, you are eating and drinking God's judgment upon yourself. That is why many of you are weak and sick and some have even died.
>
> But if we would examine ourselves, we would not be judged by God in this way.
>
> I CORINTHIANS 11:29-31

These are ultraserious words—some of the most important truths related to worship in the entire Bible. Maybe at times we don't take the admonition to clean up our lives all that seriously as we take the elements of the Lord's Table. Let me assure you, the Lord does! If there's one thing that nauseates Him, it's a lukewarm, careless attitude toward sacred things (see Revelation 3:15-17).

This was the serious illness lingering in the church at Corinth. But—here's the contrast—in verse 31, we are instructed to examine ourselves. While again we have the English word *examine*, it's from a different Greek word. This word is *diakrino*, not *dokimazo*. *Diakrino* means "to evaluate by paying careful attention to something."

Let me illustrate what this means. It's what you do every morning after a long night's sleep. You walk into the bathroom, click on the light, and look at the monstrosity reflected in the mirror. Your hair looks like it's gone through a mattress explosion, and your face is hanging low in places. Your breath is bad. Your teeth feel like they're covered with a thin layer of moss. You recognize that staying in those pajamas would start a riot. What have you done here? You've done a quick *examination* of your true condition. You don't turn the light off and say, "I'm just going to go to church like this." No. You think, *I've got to do something about this . . . and it's going to take a while.* I've got news for you: the older you get, the longer it takes for you to get yourself in shape! As I've heard all my life, "If the barn needs painting, *paint it!*" How did you know you needed to change these things? You looked in the mirror.

Every time you look into the pages of the Bible, think of each page as a mirror. God's Word convicts us of our sinful habits and offensive tendencies. We must respond by doing something about it. Again, that's application. We're applying what we've read or observed. If we don't do that, we walk away from the nutritious, healthy Scriptures without tasting them. Without application, we miss the nourishment for our lives. We don't want to sit down, read a little text, and smell the aroma but leave the meal cold on the plate—untouched, uneaten, and undigested.

I repeat: the Bible was not given to satisfy idle curiosity; it was given to transform our lives. God's desire is that we probe, observe, examine, evaluate, and determine what's genuine to make a careful decision regarding areas of our lives that need our attention. Far too many people fail to apply the Scriptures, which explains why some believers live with a sour attitude even though they've known the Lord for decades. Friends and family want them to climb to a new level of maturity, but they resist it.

Careful study mixed with application of the Scriptures will

change our attitudes—it really will! How? The Spirit of God is at work in each area of our lives through His Word. He knows us and wants us to become more and more like His Son. God's overall game plan is clear: that we become like Christ. Application accelerates that process.

APPLYING THE SCRIPTURES

This is a good time to practice applying a passage of Scripture together. Let's start with Psalm 139. This psalm is an ancient hymn composed of four stanzas, with six verses in each stanza. If you have room in the margin of your Bible, write down these four summary statements for each stanza. For verses 1-6, write, "God knows me." This is called the doctrine of omniscience. God knows everything, and that includes everything about you. How do we know that? Because we observe what the verses are saying:

> O Lord, you have examined my heart
> and know everything about me.
> You know when I sit down or stand up.
> You know my thoughts even when I'm far away.
> You see me when I travel
> and when I rest at home.
> You know everything I do.
>
> PSALM 139:1-3

Notice that the psalm begins with these words: "O Lord, you." That immediately tells us that this psalm is a prayer. The direct address "Lord" appears again and again (verses 4 and 21). "O God" appears in verses 17, 19, and 23. Throughout this hymn, David the psalmist is praying, "O Lord" and "O God." David composed this hymn and wrote it in his journal, and then it eventually found its way into the psalter, the Jews' ancient hymnbook.

As we study verse 2, we see what the doctrine of omniscience means. God knows everything about everyone and everything. You will never hear from heaven, "Would you look at that! Why, I didn't know that! Gabriel, come here and take a look! What on earth is going on?" No, that's never God's response. He knows everything, which means He never learns anything. People sometimes pray to God as if they need to inform Him of what's going on. He knows all about us, so we don't need to inform God of anything. He sees when we travel and when we're at rest.

> You know what I am going to say
>> even before I say it, LORD.
> You go before me and follow me.
>> You place your hand of blessing on my head.
> Such knowledge is too wonderful for me,
>> too great for me to understand!
>
> PSALM 139:4-6

Notice that God knows what we're going to say before we ever say it. Don't you wish you knew what you were going to say ahead of time? How often we blurt things out and later think, *Why did I ever say that?* I have a friend who puts it well: "I never felt sorry for the things I did *not* say." The psalmist underscores in verses 1-6 that God knows us.

For verses 7-12, mark in the margin of your Bible, "God is with me." Let's look back at the hymn:

> I can never escape from your Spirit!
>> I can never get away from your presence!
> If I go up to heaven, you are there;
>> if I go down to the grave, you are
>>> there.

If I ride the wings of the morning,
    if I dwell by the farthest oceans,
even there your hand will guide me,
    and your strength will support me.

PSALM 139:7-10

This stanza introduces us to the doctrine of God's omnipres-
ence, meaning that He's everywhere at one time and at the same
time. David describes the omnipresence of God by showing that
everywhere we go, God is already there. Pause and think: we are
gleaning all of this directly from the Scriptures. How faithful of
our heavenly Father to reveal so much about Himself to us! God's
Word is a reservoir of all-important information.

David uses several examples to illustrate God's presence. In
verse 9, he writes about "the wings of the morning." Your Bible
version may read "the wings of the dawn." I love the way this is
expressed—such beautiful poetry! "The wings of the dawn" refers
to the rays of light that come from the sun early in the morning.
Did you know that these beams of light travel to earth at 186,000
miles a second? If we could travel that quickly, we would arrive on
the surface of the moon in three seconds!

This phrase in verse 9 reminds me of the race between the
United States and the Soviet Union to get into space during the
Cold War. A report from the Kremlin surfaced after their first space
flight saying that they had traveled into space but did not see God.
The late pastor W. A. Criswell from First Baptist Church of Dallas
gave this classic response: "If he had stepped out of that spacesuit,
he would have seen God!" Dr. Criswell was right—God is there. He
made the planets, along with every single star. His majestic presence encompasses every galaxy.

When we apply that truth personally, it also serves as a reminder
that no matter where we find ourselves, including the most remote

or insignificant island in the sea, God is there, awaiting our arrival. If we were to escape to that tiny spot, hoping to hide from the consequences of some crime we'd committed, God would be right there. If we dragged a guilty conscience with us when we left, we'd find a guilty conscience when we arrived. As this verse is applied, we realize why travel will never bring us peace if we're at odds with the living God. As verse 7 affirms, we can never escape from His Spirit. We can never get away from His presence.

Look at the next two verses:

> I could ask the darkness to hide me
> and the light around me to become night—
> but even in darkness I cannot hide from you.
> To you the night shines as bright as day.
> Darkness and light are the same to you.

PSALM 139:11-12

Did you ever try to hide from danger as a kid? If you were afraid of the bogeyman, you might have pulled the covers over your head and thought, *He can't find me because I'm under the covers!* Growing up doesn't erase our desire to escape reality. Those on the run say to themselves, *God can't find me. I'm having this affair, but nobody will ever know about it.* This psalm assures us that God knows all about everything. There's no secret with the living God. Nothing is obscure to Him. We may run, but we cannot hide.

As we continue through this ancient but profoundly personal hymn, we arrive at the third stanza, verses 13-18. In the margin of your Bible write, "God made me." This is a reminder that God is omnipotent—He is all powerful. If you wonder when life begins, you need to make an in-depth study of Psalm 139:13-18 and then judge for yourself. The Bible reveals the truth, so let's let truth

speak. You may even want to read these six verses aloud. Pause
after each verse and picture the scene in your mind. Your life began
when you were in your mother's womb:

> You made all the delicate, inner parts of my body
>> and knit me together in my mother's womb.
> Thank you for making me so wonderfully complex!
>> Your workmanship is marvelous—how well I know it.
> You watched me as I was being formed in utter
>> seclusion,
>> as I was woven together in the dark of the womb.
> You saw me before I was born.
>> Every day of my life was recorded in your book.
> Every moment was laid out
>> before a single day had passed.

> How precious are your thoughts about me, O God.
>> They cannot be numbered!
> I can't even count them;
>> they outnumber the grains of sand!
> And when I wake up,
>> you are still with me!

PSALM 139:13-18

OVERVIEW OF PSALM 139	
Verses	**Summary**
1-6	God knows me.
7-12	God is with me.
13-18	God made me.
19-24	God, search me.

Back in the days of King David, no camera was in existence to probe into this intimate space. But God is capable of invading that space. By application, these verses are saying that when we were smaller than the size of a period at the end of a sentence—in embryonic form, only microscopic cells—God was there. He put us together, giving each of us a unique face, as well as an individual personality. While putting us together, He created our bones and made them a part of our bodily structures.

It doesn't matter if you're tall or short. It doesn't matter what your face looks like. Your loving Creator-God made you who you are. Don't worry about your identity or complain about your body. God made you . . . starting in the womb. These verses lead to one definitive message: God cares about you! The beauty of application is that it allows the print on the page to speak directly and person-ally to us. Suddenly we realize how meaningful Scripture can be.

The final stanza, consisting of six verses, is saying, "God, search me." These verses underscore the compassion of God. He is all caring! The conclusion of this last section is powerful—and very personal. Look at verses 23-24:

> Search me, O God, and know my heart;
> > test me and know my anxious thoughts.
> Point out anything in me that offends you,
> > and lead me along the path of everlasting life.
>
> PSALM 139:23-24

David isn't saying "you" and "your" anymore; it's now "me." "Search me." This is where David applies what he has just written. The psalm-ist has unpacked all this great theology: the omniscience, omnipres-ence, omnipotence, and compassion of our great God. And now he says, "O God, I need help. So search *me*." He concludes by inviting the living Lord to expose any area of his life that needs to change.

TIPS FOR APPLYING YOURSELF

The application of Scripture isn't something you need a pastor for—it's something you can do every day, during your own time with the Lord. Here are some helpful principles for you to remember when you begin to apply the Scriptures.

1. **Think.** When you apply the Scriptures, reflect on what is going on in your life. You may be worried about something. Your spouse may have recently walked out on you. You may have lost your job. You may be struggling with deep insecurity or enduring a bout of depression. You may find it difficult to get along with someone you're working with. The list could go on and on. When you begin to think about your life, ask yourself a few questions. Are there any secrets you're hiding? Face up to them. God knows it all, remember? Are there habits you're forming that are hurting you? Are there attitudes you're cultivating that need to be changed? Are there selfish motives that you're denying? Look within, and be honest with yourself and God.

   I do this every time I search the Scriptures—yes, every time. Before I ever think about the people who are going to hear some message I'm preparing, I think, "O Lord, I need to open up and talk to You about these things that are happening in my life. I need help here." Or I might say, "I don't know what it is, Lord. I have some uneasy feelings inside. I'm asking You to search my heart." I don't pray that so God will know what's happening within me, because He already sees everything. I'm praying so that God will reveal the truth to me: "Show me what You see about me. Help me know to know why I'm facing so much anxiety. Why can't I sleep? Why do I wake up feeling burdened? Why am I not able to get along with so-and-so? What are the unnecessary anchors

I'm dragging? Search me, O God." Think about what's going on in your life and ask God to reveal whatever impurities linger in your heart. Start there—with your thoughts.

2. **Acknowledge.** Identify any personal trouble spot in your life. Hebrews 12:1 refers to this as a "sin that so easily trips us up." These are sins that plague us and frequently cause us to stumble in our walks with Christ. As you're inviting the Lord to search your life and help you understand your anxious heart, be ready to acknowledge the truth of what He reveals. Maybe you need to come to terms with an area of pride, greed, selfishness, impatience, procrastination, sloth, envy, jealousy, or lust. Perhaps you are harboring an unforgiving spirit or a spirit of entitlement that has led you to think, *I've got this coming. They owe it to me.* God will unveil the truth as you apply His Word. He will also show you how you must be broken and humble before Him. When you appropriately apply the Scriptures and God probes into your inner life, the pain can be severe.

A. W. Tozer put it best: "It is doubtful whether God can bless a man greatly until He has hurt him deeply."[16] That's why for some people it takes a serious injury or surgery to get our attention. For others it's a jail sentence or a major accident. Suddenly we're made aware of our fallibility. When it comes to the application of the Scriptures, acknowledge any trouble spot. Don't try to hide from the truth or act like it doesn't exist. We need to face it head on.

3. **Ask.** Bring up specific questions as you invite the Lord to probe within. The key word here is *specific.* When you ask specific questions, you will get specific answers. Here are some examples:

> Is there a change of direction I need to make?
> Is there a promise from God's Word I need to claim?
> Is there a prayer I need to offer?
> Is there a sin I need to confess?
> Is there a verse I should memorize?
> Is there a command I need to obey?
> Is there a habit (perhaps an addiction) I need to break?
> Is there a challenge I need to stop running from?
> Is there a fear I need to overcome?
> Is there a person I need to forgive?
> Is there someone I've offended and with whom I need to make things right?

To quote Dr. Hendricks again, "Guard against the slimy ooze of indefiniteness." A prayer that casually states, "Lord, show me whatever I need to know" accomplishes little. Ask specifically. Also, get rid of the clichés and meaningless generalities in your prayers, and speak from your heart. Most of all, when you ask, be ready to face reality. The best students of the Scriptures are vulnerable and unguarded.

I remember the words of the late Lorne Sanny, when he was serving as president of the Navigators. He was ministering on the campus of the Air Force Academy. One of the top cadets in the academy, the student body president, was also a Christian—a young man others admired. Sanny was leading a small group Bible study that this young man was a member of. Sanny looked directly at him and said, "Tell us when you get alone with the Lord. When do you have your quiet time?" The cadet blushed, looked down, and then looked into the face of the president of the Navigators. "Sir, in all honesty, I don't have a quiet time," he said. "I've been faking it for years. I rarely meet alone with the Lord."

Lorne paused, swallowed hard, and then thanked the young man for being honest.

Would you be gutsy enough to say that in front of your peers? Would you honestly say, "You know, I'm very difficult to live with. I've got a raging temper. If folks only knew . . ." It's that kind of honesty the Lord loves. Acknowledge your sin and ask for help with it. When you apply the Scriptures, you will be able to face whatever temptation plagues you.

4. **Pursue.** Seek out paths that lead you to wholeness and spiritual health. I draw this application directly from the last verse of this grand psalm: "Point out anything in me that offends you, and lead me along the path of everlasting life" (Psalm 139:24).

There's something significant in that closing sentence I don't want you to miss. Go back and read the opening words in David's request: "Point out anything in me that offends you." Your Bible may read "any wicked way." The New American Standard Bible says, "See if there be any hurtful way in me." The New English Translation says, "See if there is any idolatrous tendency in me."

The Hebrew word that is translated "offense" or "hurt" is akin to the word for "idol." The phrase is *derek-ohtzeb*, which means "any way that leads to grief or pain." When we have unforgiving spirits, we're turned over to inner feelings of torment (see Matthew 18:34-35). In Psalm 139:24, David is asking the Lord to show him the path that has led to that torturing—the path that has removed inner peace. As we apply the Scriptures, we come to terms with truths like this. We seek paths that get us out of whatever miserable rut we find ourselves in. I love that the psalmist ends his composition in such a personal way.

CHARLES R. SWINDOLL

When it comes to applying Scripture, you need to be intentional
about finding ways to change the direction of your life. Ideally,
you will find someone to hold you accountable. It's impossible
to live a fully mature Christian life in isolation. We're meant to
work alongside others and mature in community. That's why close
relationships are absolutely vital. You might also keep a journal. It's
different from a diary, which is simply a record of your actions. A
journal, in contrast, focuses on what the Lord is doing within you
and what He is revealing to you.

Application starts with two commitments on your part:

> **Make certain you've trusted in Christ and placed Him
  on the throne of your life.** Tell Him you want Him to be
  at the core. Earlier in this chapter, I explained the gospel
  to you; make sure you've acted upon it. Make sure the
  One who died on the cross is your Savior. You may want
  to acknowledge that by writing your commitment in
  your journal: "This day I trust in the Lord Jesus Christ as
  my own Savior." You may also want to tell someone you
  love about the commitment you made. Follow through
  by making certain you have Christ in the center of your
  life, reigning supreme and occupying first place.

> **Start your own study of the Scriptures.** So far, you've
  been studying with me in this series. Now, with
  application, it becomes your turn. Choose a passage of
  Scripture to study. If you're not sure where to begin, you
  may want to start with the Gospel of John—perhaps
  the third chapter. Or you may choose a few proverbs to
  study every day. You may also choose to start in Genesis
  or in one of Paul's short letters. Take your time—there's
  no hurry. Take each step carefully: observe, interpret,
  correlate, and apply. Trust me on this: if you make this

commitment and stay with it, you will not remain the same person. I'll add here that you will also become a great encouragement to your pastor.

One of the greatest heartbreaks any pastor must deal with is ministering to the same people in a congregation week after week, month after month, year after year, and observing that there is no visible, lasting change in many of them. So many are still walking in the flesh. So many seek their own ways. These are indications that the truth of God's Word is not being applied. If this describes you, I urge you to break ranks. It's time for a much-needed change. Today—this very day—start applying God's Word personally. Remember: it's never too late to start doing what is right.

No one would ever think of cooking a great meal and then not serving it. We naturally pay close attention to how the food we're cooking tastes. The taste is one of the most important parts of eating. That's what all the preparation is about and why we're so careful to season the food appropriately. Just the right seasoning results in just the right taste.

The bottom line of application is this: the message of the Scriptures must grip us personally. Application is the crowning achievement of Bible study. We as believers are called to live out the message of Christ in our lives. Conviction must lead to repentance, followed by obedient action. And then comes the exciting part: putting everything together to serve the feast. That's where we're going next.

Let the feast begin!

Now that you've looked at the importance of adding the right spices to create the perfect taste, it's time to move into the kitchen and try it for yourself. The application of Scripture is the result of your observations, interpretations, and correlations. Here are some exercises to help you begin:

1. The apostle Paul gives specific instructions about Christian behavior to the church in Ephesus. Read Ephesians 4:17-32. Pray for the Holy Spirit to make these verses clear to you, and then begin the process of Bible study.

   First, take time to observe this passage very carefully. Write down some specific details that seem most important.

   Second, use your Bible tools to help you correctly interpret Paul's message to the church. What does this passage mean? What truths are being communicated here?

   Third, find other passages with similar commands and

correlate them with Ephesians 4:17-32. (For example, check out 1 Corinthians 5.)

Finally, write out how Paul's commands in Ephesians 4:17-32 apply directly to your life. Be specific. As these verses speak into your life, don't hesitate to be painfully honest!

2. Which of Paul's commands are particularly convicting for you? What steps will you take to correct and change your behavior? As you pray for the Spirit to convict you and as you apply God's Word, find someone you trust to hold you accountable.

3. Go back and review your observations, interpretations, and correlations about John 3. What can we learn from the dialogue between Jesus and Nicodemus? Come up with two different applications from the chapter.

4. In Luke 10:37, Jesus applies His parable of the Good Samaritan for us. Review your observations, interpretations, and correlations for this parable. With Jesus' application

from Luke 10:37 in mind, to whom can you show love and mercy this week?

5. Review your study of Philippians 4:4-9, and then work on three appropriate applications from this passage. How do the apostle Paul's commands play out in your own life?

6. Think about the circumstances in your life right now, and ask God to reveal any spiritual impurities that linger in your heart. Maybe you need to come to terms with an area of pride, greed, selfishness, impatience, procrastination, sloth, envy, jealousy, or lust. Remember to ask these questions:

> Is there a change of direction I need to make?
> Is there a promise from God's Word I need to claim?
> Is there a prayer I need to offer?
> Is there a sin I need to confess?
> Is there a verse I should memorize?
> Is there a command I need to obey?
> Is there a habit (perhaps an addiction) I need to break?
> Is there a challenge I need to stop running from?
> Is there a fear I need to overcome?
> Is there a person I need to forgive?
> Is there someone I've offended and with whom I need to make things right?

Ask God to search your heart and reveal what needs attention. From now on, whenever He convicts you of something from the Scriptures that addresses a sin or an issue in your life that needs to be confessed and forgiven, pause right there and deal with it. Confess your transgression to your heavenly Father. He is "the God of all grace," and He will hear you and cleanse you (1 Peter 5:10, NIV). How important it is that those presenting His Word do so with clean hands and cleansed hearts!

STAGE THREE

Serving the Feast

CHAPTER 8

SETTING THE TABLE

Preparing to Dig into God's Word

PREPARATION IS IMPORTANT, regardless of your goal. Whether
you're giving a speech in front of a crowd or playing a musical
instrument in a recital, there's no question: you need to be well
prepared. The same is true if you want to host a grand banquet.
Even if you want to serve a nice meal for a few close friends, some
planning will be required.

We've already seen that searching the Scriptures involves diligent work and attention to details. There is no shortcut, no ninety-
day-wonder formula when it comes to being a careful student of
the Bible. It takes time, and we must prepare well.

I was reminded of the value of preparation when I read about a
little boy who was born with a frail body and a debilitating speech
impediment. When he was seven, he lost his father, who had

187

meant the world to him. Things got even worse when the large inheritance his father had left for him was stolen by his guardians. Instead of watching over him, they refused to pay his tutors, depriving him of the fine education he was entitled to. To complicate matters, he wasn't able to distinguish himself in the one place that was considered of utmost significance in his culture: the floor of the Greek gymnasium.

The odds seemed to be stacked against this fatherless, frail, awkward child whom no one could understand and no one cared about. He was the last person anyone would have guessed would one day hold the power to mobilize his nation by his voice alone.

In his pathetic condition, the boy listened to a great orator speaking in the public square. The crowd sat in rapt attention, hanging on the orator's every word. This experience inspired and challenged the boy as nothing else had. While standing there listening, he resolved that he would do something about his long list of failures and inabilities. At that moment, he determined to take life by the throat. He believed that the key to reaching his goal was preparation.

This man was none other than Demosthenes, the renowned Athenian orator and statesman.

One writer describes his transformation this way:

To conquer his speech impediment, he devised his own strange exercises. He would fill his mouth with pebbles and practice speaking. He rehearsed full speeches into the wind or while running up steep inclines. He learned to give entire speeches with a single breath. And soon, his quiet, weak voice erupted with booming, powerful clarity.

Demosthenes locked himself away underground— literally—in a dugout he'd had built in which to study

and educate himself. To ensure he wouldn't indulge in
outside distractions, he shaved half his head so he'd be too
embarrassed to go outside. And from that point forward, he
dutifully descended each day into his study to work with his
voice, his facial expressions, and his arguments.

When he did venture out, it was to learn even more.
Every moment, every conversation, every transaction, was
an opportunity for him to improve his art. All of it aimed at
one goal: to face his enemies in court and win back what had
been taken from him. Which he did.

When he came of age, he finally filed suits against
the negligent guardians who had wronged him. . . .
Demosthenes eventually won.

Only a fraction of the original inheritance remained, but
the money had become secondary. Demosthenes's reputation
as an orator, ability to command a crowd and his peerless
knowledge of the intricacies of law, was worth more than
whatever remained of a once-great fortune.

Every speech he delivered made him stronger, every day
he stuck with it made him more determined. He could see
through bullies and stare down fear. In struggling with his
unfortunate fate, Demosthenes found his true calling: He
would be the voice of Athens.[17]

I love stories like this one, not only because they're true but also
because they show how an underdog can triumph. From the most
unlikely quarter, this man emerged and became the most significant individual in his day.

As we learn from the life of Demosthenes, preparation is absolutely essential. This concept is articulated well in the words of
two well-known communicators. Donald Grey Barnhouse, a well-
known expositor from the twentieth century, said, "If I had only

three years to serve the Lord, I would spend two of them studying and preparing."[18] When evangelist Billy Graham was interviewed by a reporter and asked if there was anything he would do differently if he could live his life over again, he replied, "Yes, I would have studied more and spoken less. At least three times more than I had done."[19] These statements remind me of this Chinese proverb: "Dig the well before you are thirsty."

Searching the Scriptures takes time and requires hard work. Chances are, God won't reveal His will in cloud formations during the day or in voices around your bedroom at night. He has written His will in His Word. The more careful you are in your private study and preparation, the more competent you will become in teaching it to others.

As we learn to dig in deeply to Scripture, diligence and discipline are not optional. As with any skill, we have to put our whole hearts into it if we want to get better at it. Like Demosthenes, we must passionately and patiently prepare!

Don't think you must go to seminary to understand the Bible or to teach its truths. It isn't essential for you to learn Greek or Aramaic or Hebrew to know the Bible. Furthermore, you don't have to be brilliant or creative to know the Bible. You just have to spend time preparing, studying, praying, and giving your attention to Scripture.

If you have learned each step of studying the Scriptures—observation, interpretation, correlation, and application—that's great news! But it's not enough to be content with your personal growth and stop there. Now it's time for you to share your knowledge with other people. You may not be called to preach behind a pulpit or teach a class or write a book, but you can still open up the Scriptures with others, even if it's in a small group or a one-on-one setting.

THE MEANING OF EXPOSITION

Let's start with a definition of *exposition*. Exposition is the process of learning and explaining the meaning and purpose of a given text. This might happen in a sermon, in a classroom, in a small group setting, or around the dinner table—wherever people are reading and applying a passage of Scripture.

> It occurs when the biblical text is carefully observed, clearly understood, and interestingly explained.
> It occurs when the text remains the central focus of attention throughout the delivery of a message.
> It occurs when the text is illustrated and applied in keeping with today's real-world needs.

If you want to be a trustworthy expositor, there are some key principles you need to keep in mind:

> Stay with the text (that's focus).
> Make certain your comments square with the Scriptures (that's accuracy).
> Use terms that even the uninitiated can understand (that's clarity).
> Remain sensitive to your audience and connect with them (that's practicality).
> Be real and, when necessary, unguarded and vulnerable (that's authenticity).

Those are good checkpoints with which to grade any lesson that is taught or sermon that is preached. Did the pastor or teacher literally observe the Scriptures for the purpose of understanding and explaining them? When the message was delivered, was it based on the Word of God, not someone's opinion or personal ideas? Did the message resonate with power and authority? Did it hold the listeners' attention? Lastly, was it applied and illustrated in a way that the audience could understand?

All my sermons pass through these gates in my mind. I want my teaching and preaching to be accurate, clear, relevant, and practical. To make that happen, I must be accurate with the biblical text. I must speak clearly and explain the Scriptures so anyone, not just mature Christians, can understand. I decode what could be confusing by clarifying difficult or unusual terms. Then I ask, "Is it relevant? Am I helping the hearer realize how relevant God's Word is?" And then, as it is applied, I ask, "Is it practical? Am I giving listeners something they can take with them the rest of the week?" That last question is the acid test of exposition. The purpose of the Bible is not to fill our heads with knowledge but to fill our lives with truth and grace. Our study of Scripture should enable us to live out the life of Christ before others, who are "reading" His gospel through the way we live.

Notice that with this introduction to the term *exposition*, I haven't addressed essentials like pace or creativity or word pictures or humor. Nor have I mentioned harmful techniques like manipulation, authoritarianism, legalism, and the misuse of guilt. Just as the presentation of a meal influences how the meal tastes, the presentation of the Scriptures affects how it is received by the listener. A gourmet feast served on paper plates with plastic utensils is less appealing and therefore less appreciated. A simple frozen meal, quickly reheated but served on ornate china, also doesn't fit together. Preparation of the biblical text requires careful presentation of the meaning as well as precise, pertinent application. We must learn to set the table to match the occasion. This is part of the preparation process.

Let's review those four familiar steps of the process and go a little deeper as we consider these terms in the context of teaching.

TEACHING THROUGH OBSERVATION

First, we read what the verse says and observe the context. As we've learned, every verse fits into a specific context. Guard against isolating one verse and having it stand all alone. That's like rushing through a magazine article, pulling out one sentence, and jumping to a conclusion about the message of the entire article. Just as you must read all of an article to understand it, you must read the context of a verse to grasp its meaning. That's called integrating the verse with its context.

Imagine if I told you the story of Demosthenes but began when he puts pebbles in his mouth. You'd ask, "What in the world is that about?" Without knowing the setting of Demosthenes's story, you wouldn't understand the purpose behind his unusual method of teaching himself to speak.

I once stuttered terribly. I remember going into middle school paralyzed by the thought of speaking in public. By the time I began high school, my stuttering was creating some serious consequences. I'll never forget our drama and speech teacher in high school—a man named Dick Nieme. I still remember the day he walked up to me in the hallway during my freshman year. He looked at me and said, "I want you in my debate class. I also want you to be a part of our drama team." I honestly thought he was talking to the guy beside me at the next locker.

When I realized he was addressing me, my response was, "M-m-m-me? You want . . . you want m-m-me to . . . to . . . to d-d-do that?" I'm not exaggerating.

He said, "Yeah. You've got it."

I thought, *I know I've got it—that's my problem. What I need to do is to get rid of it!* When I finally got my protest out, he replied, "Well, that's why I'm here."

The summer before classes started the following year, he met with me and gave me speech lessons. Ultimately, he taught me how to speak without stuttering. He had no idea (and I certainly had no clue) how my life would turn out and how God would use my voice as a way to serve Him.

Mr. Nieme said, "By the time I'm through and we've learned these things together, you'll have the lead in our senior play." And you know what? I did! And I didn't stutter once.

To this day, there are still words that challenge me, and I have to pace myself, remembering what Mr. Nieme taught me about my mind running ahead of my mouth. I slow down when I get to those consonants that would normally make me choke up or stutter. It took much preparation, but now I'm able to teach and preach because I learned some of those disciplines. Talk about the value of an insightful teacher!

Now let's look at a biblical example from Joshua 1. Understanding where this chapter falls in the biblical story will help us understand the context for the book of Joshua. Joshua is an intimidated man. He has been charged to fill the sandals of the greatest leader Israel had ever known. Moses was the God-appointed deliverer whom God used to lead the people out of slavery in Egypt, through the desert, and all the way to the edge of the Promised Land. Let's look at how the book of Joshua begins:

> After the death of Moses the LORD's servant, the LORD spoke to Joshua son of Nun, Moses' assistant. He said, "Moses my servant is dead. Therefore, the time has come for you to lead these people, the Israelites, across the Jordan River into the land I am giving them."
>
> JOSHUA 1:1-2

The first thing we observe in this passage is that Moses was dead. The second is that God commissioned Joshua to take Moses' place. Joshua's first task? To lead the Israelites across the Jordan River. We now ask ourselves, *Where's the Jordan River?* But you don't have to wonder—you can find it on one of the maps in the back of your Bible or in a Bible atlas. Become a student of biblical geography. The Lord told Joshua, "The time has come for you to lead these people . . . across the Jordan River." Notice that God revealed explicitly where Joshua and the Israelites were to go. He even outlined the boundaries of the Promised Land.

Read what God said next:

> I promise you what I promised Moses: "Wherever you
> set foot, you will be on land I have given you—from the
> Negev wilderness in the south to the Lebanon mountains
> in the north, from the Euphrates River in the east to the
> Mediterranean Sea in the west, including all the land of the
> Hittites."
>
> JOSHUA 1:3-4

Joshua was going to lead an invasion—the Israelites were going to fight for the land. Joshua knew that the Lord had already given the land to him and the rest of the Israelites.

Where is this land? Again, check the map. To the south you will find the Negev wilderness. The word *Negev* means "desert." How do I know that? From consulting my Bible dictionary. You don't have to know Hebrew; just look up *Negev*, and you'll find the meaning. Next, look to the north, all the way to the Lebanon Mountains. That's the northern border. The eastern border is marked by the Euphrates River. If you go west, you'll find the Great Sea, which is the Mediterranean. The borders of the Promised Land are clearly defined. The Negev to the south, the Lebanon Mountains to the north, the Euphrates River to the east, and the Mediterranean Sea to the west. God promised all that land to His people.

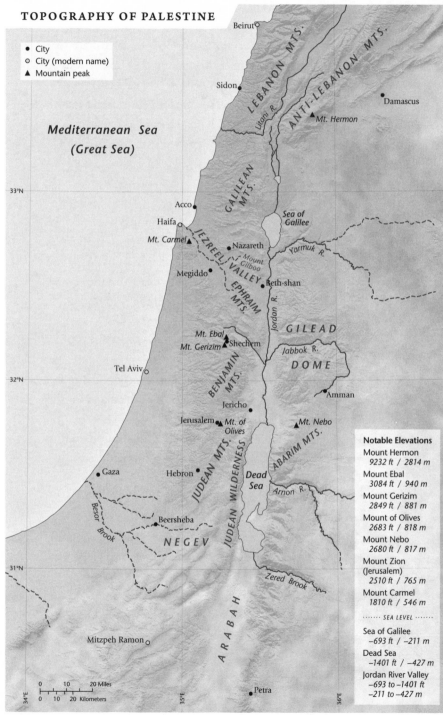

TOPOGRAPHY OF PALESTINE

- ● City
- ○ City (modern name)
- ▲ Mountain peak

Mediterranean Sea
(Great Sea)

Beirut ○

Sidon ●

Damascus ●

LEBANON MTS.

ANTI-LEBANON MTS.

Litani R.

▲ Mt. Hermon

33°N

Acco ●

Haifa ○

Mt. Carmel ▲

GALILEAN MTS.

Sea of Galilee

JEZREEL VALLEY

Nazareth ●

Mount Gilboa

Megiddo ●

Yarmuk R.

Beth-shan ●

EPHRAIM MTS.

Jordan R.

GILEAD

Mt. Ebal ▲

Mt. Gerizim ▲ Shechem ●

Jabbok R.

DOME

Tel Aviv ○

BENJAMIN MTS.

32°N

Amman ●

Jericho ●

Jerusalem ● Mt. of Olives ▲

▲ Mt. Nebo

ABARIM MTS.

Gaza ●

Hebron ●

JUDEAN MTS.

Dead Sea

JUDEAN WILDERNESS

Arnon R.

Besor Brook

Beersheba ●

NEGEV

31°N

Zered Brook

Notable Elevations

Mount Hermon
9232 ft / 2814 m

Mount Ebal
3084 ft / 940 m

Mount Gerizim
2849 ft / 881 m

Mount of Olives
2683 ft / 818 m

Mount Nebo
2680 ft / 817 m

Mount Zion (Jerusalem)
2510 ft / 765 m

Mount Carmel
1810 ft / 546 m

········ SEA LEVEL ········

Sea of Galilee
−693 ft / −211 m

Dead Sea
−1401 ft / −427 m

Jordan River Valley
−693 to −1401 ft
−211 to −427 m

Mitzpeh Ramon ○

ARABAH

0   10   20 Miles
0   10   20 Kilometers

34°E   35°E   36°E

Petra ●

Now that we have the geography down, it's time to look into the conquest. The Lord knew how difficult the enemy would be. They were the Hittites, and they were as mean as a pack of junkyard dogs. And they were entrenched in the land promised to Israel. How do I know that? Again, my Bible dictionary provides those details when I look up *Hittites*. Now read what the Lord promised:

No one will be able to stand against you as long as you live.
For I will be with you as I was with Moses. I will not fail you
or abandon you.
JOSHUA 1:5

God was saying, in effect, "That's My promise, Joshua, and you can take it to the bank!" Can you see the value of context in this passage of Scripture? Now we know the big-picture boundaries, the specific objective (the conquest), and the divine promise. All of that is packed into verses 3-5.

Next, we find God's challenge to Joshua in verses 6-9:

Be strong and courageous, for you are the one who will
lead these people to possess all the land I swore to their
ancestors I would give them. Be strong and very courageous.
Be careful to obey all the instructions Moses gave you. Do
not deviate from them, turning either to the right or to the
left. Then you will be successful in everything you do. Study
this Book of Instruction continually. Meditate on it day and
night so you will be sure to obey everything written in it.
Only then will you prosper and succeed in all you do. This
is my command—be strong and courageous! Do not be
afraid or discouraged. For the LORD your God is with you
wherever you go.
JOSHUA 1:6-9

Verses 6 and 7 repeat the command: "Be strong and [very] courageous." Again, verse 9 says, "Be strong and courageous!" Then the same command reemerges in the last verse of the chapter:

> Anyone who rebels against your orders and does not obey
> your words and everything you command will be put to
> death. So be strong and courageous!
> JOSHUA 1:18

Repetition in the narrative indicates that we've come across some significant terms. In this case, that means you need to check the meaning of *strong* and the meaning of *courageous*. When you're studying a passage of Scripture, you want to develop a definition of what the key words mean. You will need a Bible dictionary to do so. You might spend thirty or forty minutes investigating these words as you check definitions and write them in your journal or in the margin of your Bible.

If you want to get to know the Bible, it's crucial that you write down the results of your study. If you want to teach the Scriptures, your personal notes will play a vital role in your teaching. You'll cultivate your ability to teach by disciplining yourself to study the context, the meaning of words, the definitions, the locations, and other important details. All of this preparation adds depth to your exposition.

TEACHING THROUGH INTERPRETATION

The next step of Bible study is interpretation. Remember, when the Lord writes something four times in one chapter of His Word, it's there for a reason. Interpretation helps us investigate why He would repeat, "Be strong and courageous" four times. Apparently Joshua felt fearful—more than a little intimidated.

During my fifty-plus years in ministry, I've stepped into the shoes of some very influential people. Back in 1967, I left a church in New England and became the pastor of Irving Bible Church in Irving, Texas. Dr. Stanley Toussaint, who had taught me Greek in seminary, had been the church's former pastor. He left a significant legacy there, and the congregation loved and respected him. I was younger and less experienced, so I felt somewhat intimidated.

Today I'm the senior pastor at Stonebriar Community Church, and guess who's in the congregation. The same man, Dr. Stanley Toussaint! Believe me, when somebody has taught you as much as Dr. Toussaint taught me, it prompts you to wonder why you're at the pulpit preaching while he's sitting in the congregation! In my mind, he needs to be preaching, and I need to be in the pew. But that is God's call, not mine. I might add that Dr. Toussaint has always been affirming, gracious, and encouraging to me—a great mentor and friend.

When I returned to Dallas Theological Seminary and joined the leadership team, I sat in the seat where Dr. John Walvoord had sat for well over thirty years, followed by Dr. Donald Campbell, who served as president for eight years. After Dr. Campbell's tenure, the seminary called me to lead the school. It took a lot of convincing on their part—not to mention the powerful prompting of the Holy Spirit—for me to say yes.

I strongly resisted the call at first because I didn't feel qualified. While wrestling with what I should do, Cynthia, said to me, "I think it's a good idea."

"Whose side are you on?" I said. "I can't go there. That's where all the intellectual theological eggheads are."

"They're not looking for another theologian," she replied. "They're looking for a shepherd."

That was an insight I hadn't considered. I finally accepted, but I had to guard against the temptation to remain intimidated. Like

Joshua, who stepped into Moses' sandals, I needed to be "strong and courageous."

If you're going to teach about Joshua, you need to stand in his sandals. You need to picture being the new leader. Imagine what it must have felt like, knowing that Moses had been dead only thirty days and that although he was physically gone, he was still present in the minds of the Israelites. Up to that point, Joshua had been Moses' assistant, serving behind the scenes. Now he was to be their leader. This change would require strength and courage.

When you interpret these verses, you have to ask questions like, "Where are these locations? Who are the Hittites? What's the difference between *strong* and *courageous*?" And with some imagination, "How must Joshua have felt?" You must diligently seek out the pertinent information in your biblical resources, as well as through your own sanctified imagination. Allow it to roam here and there. Imagine feelings, conversations, and struggles. As you do so, the people and events on the pages of Scripture will come to life.

TEACHING THROUGH CORRELATION

This brings us to correlation. Correlation, as you'll recall, is discovering what the Bible says elsewhere about the same or similar subjects. We're focusing on the words God gave Joshua when it was time for him to take over leadership. At this point, he had not yet led the people; God was still preparing him. The secret of leadership is the same secret for delivering truths about God's Word or developing godly character: preparation. God was preparing Joshua for what was in front of him. There are a number of places where God addresses preparation in ways that parallel Joshua 1:6-8:

> > In Deuteronomy 1, God commands the Israelites to leave Mount Sinai and appoint the necessary leadership.

> In Deuteronomy 11:22-24, God calls Israel to obey, love, and serve Him using similar words to Joshua 1.
> In Judges 1, the people fail to follow through with everything the Lord commanded them to do under Joshua. Instead of driving out all the Canaanites, they put up with an enemy that eventually became a thorn in their side. They didn't do exactly what they were commanded to do by Joshua; they were neither strong nor courageous.

These corresponding passages help us see how Joshua 1 is similar to previous passages and also what happened after the people didn't obey. Correlation always broadens our knowledge of the subject and helps us understand Scripture on a deeper, broader level.

TEACHING THROUGH APPLICATION

Finally, we come to application, the crowning step. It's also my favorite part, because application has to do with determining what these verses mean for me and what they could mean for others. First we ask, "Does this apply to something in my life or in another person's life?" We all deal with fear and intimidation at some point. You may have gone to the doctor this week and received some results that are making you uneasy. What the Bible says about Joshua could be said to anyone who is facing fear. If you are in need of courage, you'll be able to identify with the challenge Joshua faced. Maybe you're stepping into the shoes of a successful leader, and now it's your turn to lead. Your predecessor is gone, but his or her voice is in the woodwork. You can apply this passage to that situation.

These connections all happen by way of application. Here are some applicable principles we can draw from a section of Scripture. First, A. W. Tozer said that *nothing of God dies when a man of God dies.*[20] I draw that principle from Joshua 1:1-9. Moses was dead, and Joshua was going to take over leadership. Nothing of God died. I may apply this principle by asking, "Have you lost someone who meant the world to you? Quite likely you have. It may have been your spouse, your child, a parent, or a close friend. But be assured of this: nothing of God has died."

I don't know how many times at funerals I've had the living spouse say to me, "I wish I could have died with her [or him]." I do my best to say tactfully, "Think of it this way. The same God who watched over your loved one's death has chosen to leave you here. He knows what He's doing. Nothing of God dies when a man or woman of God dies. He is still the same God. He plans to use you in a new and different way now. God is not *almost* sovereign. He has intentionally allowed you to live for the reasons He will reveal to you."

Another principle we can glean from this passage is that *halfhearted obedience leads to wholehearted disobedience.* Truth be told, there is no such thing as halfhearted obedience. Either we are obedient or we're not. Sometimes we rationalize and say, "Well, I've kept several of God's commands but not all of them." Then you broke all the commands. That's why God says, "Do not deviate from them, turning either to the right or to the left." Look back at Joshua 1:7:

> Be strong and very courageous. Be careful to obey all the instructions Moses gave you. Do not deviate from them, turning either to the right or to the left. Then you will be successful in everything you do.

Another important principle is that *deviation results in devastation.* God made this clear to Joshua by reminding him not to waver from his call. Joshua's success was based on his faithfulness to his God.

I must add this note about application: crucial questions should accompany application. For example, you might ask, "Is there some important decision I need to make?" Here's another one: "How can I turn my fears and anxiety into trust?" Perhaps you've

been wasting your time in fear and churning in anxiety. You've
been worrying and struggling with this or that. You know you
need to realize that the Lord is with you wherever you go and that
He has never abandoned you. Ask yourself, "What must I do to
remember that?"

I'm reminded of how great God's love is for us from the prophet
Isaiah. How about memorizing these soothing words?

> Can a mother forget her nursing child?
>   Can she feel no love for the child she has borne?
> But even if that were possible,
>   I would not forget you!
> See, I have written your name on the palms of my hands.
>
> ISAIAH 49:15-16

Isn't that a great passage of Scripture? It's worth looking at again.
Notice that it's right out of Isaiah's journal! It's as if God is saying
to us: "I know exactly where you are." You may have lost your job.
You may not even have a car. You may feel like you've been abandoned. But don't dwell there. You have an omnipotent God who
knows all things. In fact, your ways are continually before Him. He
has a plan for you, and it's filled with hope. He will never give up
on you. Peter reminds his churches of this key truth:

> The Lord isn't really being slow about his promise, as some
> people think. No, he is being patient for your sake. He does not
> want anyone to be destroyed, but wants everyone to repent.
>
> 2 PETER 3:9

Isn't that a great thought? This reminder of God's desire for our
salvation brings me to another crucial question: Do you need to
accept Christ as your own Savior? Do you need to trust the Lord

Jesus, who died on the cross and paid the penalty for your sin in full? You've likely heard messages like this before—perhaps many times in your life. But have you ever trusted Him personally?

Maybe the ultimate application at the end of this section is simply, "I need to trust God. I need to walk with God. I've been distant from Him for too long. I really want a relationship with Him that will last forever." When God says that He's with us always (see Matthew 28:20), He means *always*.

Applications like this one are invariably appropriate. When we teach, we must never assume that all who listen are a part of God's forever family.

SETTING THE TABLE

Once you have made your way through the process of *observing* the text, *interpreting* the passage, and *correlating* it with other Scriptures, it's easy to see the power of *application*. Part of preparation is knowing your audience or congregation well enough to present the Scriptures in a way that helps them come to terms with the truth—right where they are.

Preparing to teach or preach the Bible is much like setting a lovely table for a delicious meal. It's a vital part of the process that results in food for the soul.

Obviously, setting the table leads to the best part—eating a delicious meal. But first, you need to know how it's going to taste. As the chef who has prepared the meal, you must taste it yourself before serving it to others. The application of the biblical text always begins with the teacher or preacher. We must first apply the Scriptures to our own lives before we can challenge others to do the same. So it's time to put our meal through the "taste test." Are you ready?

Now that we've learned how to prepare a meal, it's time to set the table in a way that complements the feast about to be served. Here are some exercises that will help you prepare to teach or preach God's Word.

1. At the end of chapter 7, we worked on applying Ephesians 4:17-32. Now it's time to get ready to present what you learned. Think of a person or group you might be able to teach these truths to. Maybe it's a Sunday school class, a friend, a group at work, a small group that meets in your home, or even your own children or grandchildren. Your audience might be adults, teenagers, or children. Once you've determined who your audience is, plan how you will present the truths of Ephesians 4:17-32 to them in a way that is engaging and helpful. Here are some questions to consider:

   What can you do to help your students see the observations you made in the text?

What needs to be explained so they will understand the meaning of these verses?

What other passages should you highlight to show the correlation between Paul's commands and other Scripture passages? Would it be helpful to use an additional Bible version or a paraphrase?

What specific applications of the passage will be most helpful for your audience?

Take your time as you prepare to serve this scriptural feast. Your listeners will benefit when you patiently yet confidently lead them into the truths of Scripture.

2. Now go through the same steps with another passage that you've worked on. You can use Jesus' encounter with Nicodemus in John 3, Paul's charge to the church at Philippi in Philippians 4:4-9, or Jesus' parable of the Good Samaritan in Luke 10:25-37. Be sure to have an audience in mind to whom you can present this. Prepare whichever passage you choose by going through the questions above.

Press on with genuine enthusiasm and great anticipation. God has promised to bless the declaration of His Word—it will never return empty! Find encouragement by reading Isaiah 55:10-11.

CHAPTER 9

TASTING A SAMPLE

Learning Where We Fit in the Story

HAVE YOU EVER ATTENDED a cooking demonstration where free samples were given away? The entire process may be entertaining—watching the chef prepare the food and smelling the tantalizing aromas that waft your way—but without question, the highlight is when you actually get to taste a bite.

In making a meal fit for royalty, chefs carefully choose the seasonings, the right cut of meat, the blend of vegetables, and the delicate flavors of the dessert. They are mindful of their audience, wanting to craft something that will be satisfying, healthy, and delicious. After all the preparation that goes into making an elaborate dish, they want to be absolutely certain that everything tastes just right.

Such careful attention to detail is even more important when preparing a Bible study or a sermon that will be presented to others. But we need to ensure that we are taking in a steady diet of the Word ourselves before we can serve it to others. We must never forget what the writer of Hebrews declares:

> For the word of God is alive and powerful. It is sharper than the sharpest two-edged sword, cutting between soul and spirit, between joint and marrow. It exposes our innermost thoughts and desires.
>
> HEBREWS 4:12

The living Word of God must penetrate and probe our own souls before we present it to others. It's only after our hearts have been examined, cleansed, and softened by God and we've opened ourselves to His instruction, encouragement, rebuke, and correction that we'll be ready to teach His truths to others.

A PARABLE ABOUT PREPARATION

In Mark 4, Jesus tells a story that illustrates the importance of listening and being teachable. In order to get a feel for the setting of this story, let's talk a little about where Jesus was teaching at the time. The Mount of Beatitudes (as it is now called) is a gentle slope that emerges from the north edge of the Sea of Galilee and rises to a crest. Quite likely, the now-immortal Sermon on the Mount that Jesus delivered was presented on or near that hill. The sea forms a quiet bay on the north end, called the Bay of Parables. It's believed that when Jesus was engaged in His Galilean ministry, this is where He shared many of the parables that have found their way into the Scriptures. This is precisely where Jesus and His close friends and followers were when He shared the story recorded in Mark 4.

Interestingly, this particular terrain provided a natural amphitheater that enhanced the acoustics. Even without the use of microphones and speakers, the voice of an individual could easily be heard there among a large group. Theologian James Edwards writes, "Israeli scientists have verified that the 'Bay of Parables' can transmit a human voice effortlessly to several thousand people on shore."[21]

My longtime friend Dr. Wayne Stiles, who is a vital part of our Insight for Living ministry and a lover of the land of Israel, said that on one of his trips, he and his group tested this assertion. He stood at the shoreline and had a number of his fellow travelers gather along the slope. He said, "I spoke in just a conversational tone, and every word could be heard by those who were there."

Even more intriguing, Jesus didn't simply stand at the seashore; He got into a fishing boat, pushed away from the shoreline, and used the boat as something of a pulpit to tell His story to those who had gathered. It seems that everyone had assembled there spontaneously. No one had a scroll of the ancient Scriptures tucked under his or her arm. Most likely, the people who showed up were from around Galilee, perhaps from as far away as Jesus' boyhood home of Nazareth and maybe even from the mountainous area to the north, as far as Caesarea Philippi. All together, they formed a fairly large crowd.

Using the acoustical advantage of this hill, Jesus began to speak. Everyone loves a good story—and a good story includes intriguing characters. Our interest is piqued as the plot unfolds, eventually bringing us to an unexpected conclusion.

It's helpful to remember that in every parable there is one major spiritual lesson; we never want to miss that lesson. There may be other minor messages, but there's always one especially important lesson that may or may not be stated. This parable is no exception. With the help of our imaginations, we can almost hear Jesus' voice as He spoke from the boat in the bay.

As a boy, I remember fishing with my father and my maternal grandfather. The three of us would sit in my granddad's boat—a sixteen-foot fishing boat with a little thirty-five-horsepower

Evinrude motor fixed to the stern. Early in the morning, we'd make our way out to the middle of Carancahua Bay, which opens into Matagorda Bay and eventually leads out to the Gulf of Mexico.

Our bay was usually a quiet body of water, especially in the morning hours before dawn. When my granddad turned off the motor, we'd cast out our lines to fish. In those days, I used a long cane fishing pole. I'd drop my line in the water, and we'd sit there in silence. The water was so still that when my line landed in the water, it would make little ringlets all around it.

When water is still like that, it's called a slick. I quickly learned that when there were other boats on the water, we could hear everything people said, even though they were hundreds of yards away. (It was eavesdropping at its best.) I can still hear my father say with a smile, "Listen, Son. You'll learn a lot."

OBSERVING THE PARABLE

As we read this story in Mark 4, let's imagine how quiet it must have been as Jesus' voice carried across the calm waters. As we study, we want to observe, interpret, correlate, and apply, just as we've learned to do in this book. We'll begin by observing the Scriptures—by seeing what the verses say as Mark originally wrote them.

> Once again Jesus began teaching by the lakeshore. A very large crowd soon gathered around him, so he got into a boat. Then he sat in the boat while all the people remained on the shore.
>
> MARK 4:1

Mark tells us exactly where Jesus was: by the lakeshore. Let's pause and think about why. Maybe the crowd was so large that Jesus was pushed almost to the water's edge. He had to get into the boat to create some space between Himself and the crowd. Picture it in your mind as He steps into the boat and sits down. Jesus rarely taught standing up. In fact, to this day, rabbis often sit down to teach just like in ancient days. Next, we read:

> He taught them by telling many stories in the form of parables, such as this one.
>
> MARK 4:2

As you come across words that aren't familiar to you, it's important to check them out. If you want to know your Bible well, looking up definitions is a good way to go deeper. You will remember that *parable* comes from the Greek word *paraballo*. *Para* means "beside," and the verb *ballo* means "to place or throw." When we put the two parts together, it means "to lay by the side of; to compare so as to see the likeness or similarity."

You don't need to be a scholar to do any of this—there are books and electronic tools that provide this information. If you own a Bible dictionary, look up the word *parable*. According to *New Unger's Bible Dictionary*, this word means "to lay by the side of; to compare so as to see the likeness or similarity." Defining words is a simple step to take, but it's important as you develop your skills as a student of the Word.

When you get serious about doing your own Bible study, you will no longer be satisfied to sit with only a Bible in your lap. You'll also want to have a pad of paper so you can take notes. I do this every time I study. I use yellow tablets (I don't know why, but they have to be yellow!) and write all my notes on my tablet. From those notes, I transfer the information to my teaching lesson or sermon. It's a simple process, and you can do the same.

As I read this chapter in Mark 4, I'm thinking and learning while I'm reading. I might write down notes like these: "Jesus is by a lake. He's in a boat. A very large crowd has gathered. He sits down and begins to teach them." After I make those observations, I read Jesus' opening statement:

Listen! A farmer went out to plant some seed.
MARK 4:3

While reading, I observe that Jesus uses the word *listen*. This is a simple, basic observation, but it's valuable, so concentrate! Don't let your mind drift to a ball game or to what you're going to fix for supper or to something at work—not if you're going to get something out of the Scriptures. Pray for the ability to concentrate and pay close attention. Why? Because every word Jesus says is important. Unlike us, Jesus doesn't run down verbal rabbit trails. He doesn't use words that are redundant or superfluous. His words are significant; not one is wasted. By listening to what He's saying, we can enter into the scene. Go there! In this passage, we know that Jesus is by the shoreline and that He's teaching the people through a story. You might even read aloud, slowly and thoughtfully:

Listen! A farmer went out to plant some seed.

The agricultural world of farming may be unfamiliar to you. Many people in our world today have never farmed. I worked on a farm just long enough to know I didn't want to work on a farm for the rest of my life! It's extremely hard work. Without much farming experience, I don't know what's involved when a farmer plants seed. And I certainly have never seen how seeds were planted in the first century.

After doing some research, I found out how this was done. Since farmers didn't have any equipment or machinery for planting in Jesus' day, they would reach their hands into a bag and scatter the seed. To spread the seed all around, they would throw seed here and there as they walked along their fields. This scene was likely very familiar for a first-century audience. Jesus was placing something familiar in their minds to help them learn something unfamiliar in the spiritual realm. If you're going to teach through illustration or analogy, always start with something familiar. It may be a fish, a coin, a ball, or a mirror. Whatever it is, it should be something common and instantly familiar to your listeners. Your goal is to use it as a bridge to teach something new and unfamiliar.

I love the way Dr. Warren Wiersbe describes the parable: "Parables start off like *pictures*, then become *mirrors*, and then become *windows*. First there's *sight* as we see a slice of life in the picture; then there's *insight* as we see ourselves in the mirror; and then there's *vision* as we look through the window of revelation and see the Lord."[22]

What a helpful description! A parable eventually becomes a window, enabling us to look beyond the obvious. Through that window of understanding, we can see the Lord at work in the spiritual realm. Keep that description in mind as you read the words of Jesus.

> As he scattered it across his field, some of the seed fell on a footpath, and the birds came and ate it.
> MARK 4:4

On my tablet I would write, "First seed fell on the footpath." Picture this in your mind. We've all walked on paths in heavily traveled areas. The seed that falls on such a path would lie there on top of the hard soil, allowing birds to come and take it. On my tablet, I would write down the result Jesus mentions.

> Other seed fell on shallow soil with underlying rock. The seed sprouted quickly because the soil was shallow. But the

plant soon wilted under the hot sun, and since it didn't have deep roots, it died.

MARK 4:5-6

This second example takes us to a different planting area. There's a little bit of soil, and underneath it is solid rock. I recently saw some construction workers digging not too far from my house. The soil in our area is filled with rocks, which makes for tough digging. When I saw a pile of rocks at the site, I thought of this parable.

Farmers in the first century faced the same challenge. As they cast their seed, some of it would fall on a thin shelf of soil with rock beneath it. The seed germinates, but it doesn't take root. It lies in the shallow soil, and it doesn't take long before the plant dries out and dies. I would write all that on my tablet.

As I study, I'm starting to see a progression, which becomes clear with the mention of the third category of seed.

Other seed fell among thorns that grew up and choked out the tender plants so they produced no grain. Still other seeds fell on fertile soil, and they sprouted, grew, and produced a crop that was thirty, sixty, and even a hundred times as much as had been planted!

MARK 4:7-8

Look at verse 7, which describes the thorny soil. Jesus states that when there's a combination of seeds and thorns, the thorns win. I would write this on my tablet as well.

The fourth category represents the fertile soil. What happens here? The soil is soft, and the seed falls into it. The seed germinates, takes root, sprouts, grows, and begins to produce a crop—thirty, sixty, and one hundred times what was planted. Again, all of these observations would be recorded on my tablet.

Then he said, "Anyone with ears to hear should listen and understand."

MARK 4:9

The people in the crowd were all sitting on the slope, listening and thinking. Jesus had used a setting they were all familiar with. Maybe there was even a farmer on a nearby mound who was planting his crops. Jesus may have pointed to him and said, "You see, just as a farmer goes into a field and sows seed . . ." There are recognizable illustrations all around us.

The seventeenth-century architect Sir Christopher Wren lies buried at St. Paul's Cathedral, the great church that was designed by his own genius. On his tombstone there is a simple inscription written in Latin. It reads, when translated, "If you seek his monument, look around." If you were sitting in that great cathedral today, you'd be surrounded by his monument. Talk about a great word picture!

Jesus found numerous word pictures and truths in the common things of life, all of which are designed to lead us to the Lord, if we would only see them in the pictures He paints. With attention, these pictures ultimately become windows that reveal the Lord to us.

We can find all of this and so much more in Mark 4. If we're not careful, we'll race on to the next chapter and the next, missing most of what Jesus was teaching. Remember, the Bible doesn't yield its fruit to the hurried soul or the lazy mind. We have to pause and let the wonder in. We must also concentrate and release our imaginations. That's why He says, in effect, "Listen up! There's so much here for you."

The scene doesn't end with the story. Read on.

Later, when Jesus was alone with the twelve disciples and with the others who were gathered around, they asked him what the parables meant.

MARK 4:10

Perhaps the disciples thought, *We understand the soil. We understand the farmer. We've all seen that through our growing-up years. But we don't know what You're getting at. What's with the soil and the seed?* Gratefully, all the guesswork is taken out of the parable—for the disciples and for us.

INTERPRETING THE PARABLE

Jesus specifically answered His disciples' question about what this parable means. Often parables are difficult to figure out, but Jesus interpreted it for them, explaining the meaning plainly. Look closely:

> Then Jesus said to them, "If you can't understand the meaning of this parable, how will you understand all the other parables?"
>
> MARK 4:13

Jesus was saying there's a pattern here that's like all the other parables. So let's look for those similarities in His stories about the obvious and the familiar.

Before we go there, however, let me repeat a previous warning, especially for those who are detail minded: be careful not to make every part of the story significant. Just focus on the essentials. If you try to make the parable "walk on all fours," you'll have analysis paralysis. You'll get lost in all the details and miss what you're looking for: the main lesson.

Jesus was a master teacher. He didn't tell His listeners to "unroll the scroll," because they didn't have scrolls with them. They were sitting there listening to Him—many of them for the first time—and suddenly their minds were riveted by this story that connected with their familiar world. Jesus modeled communication at its best.

In answering their question about the meaning of the parable,

Jesus said, in effect, "Let Me help you." He didn't shame the disciples for not knowing. It's as if He said, "Now, listen carefully, and I'll unpack the story." And that's exactly what He did. He returned to the beginning of the story, explaining its spiritual message.

The farmer plants seed by taking God's word to others.

MARK 4:14

Let's pause here. Jesus mentioned the seed several times throughout the story. Notice that the seed represents the same thing regardless of where it lands. The seed is the same on thorny soil as it is on the hard path or on fertile soil. The seed doesn't change. So what is the seed? Jesus identifies it as God's Word.

When you share the message of Christ with someone else, you're planting a seed, regardless of the response. When I preach, I'm planting a seed. When good teachers stand in front of a class and share the Word of God with their students, it's like they're planting a seed, whether those in the class appreciate it or ignore it. The seed is the same no matter where it's thrown.

Let me add this admonition to all who teach God's truth: stay with the seed. Don't ever change it. Don't look for something else to plant. The seed is the Bible, the Word of God, and God promises it will never return empty (see Isaiah 55:10-11).

I love the way Dr. Steven J. Lawson talks about keeping Scripture central: "This Word-centered focus in the pulpit is the defining mark of all true expositors. Those who preach and teach the Word are to be so deeply rooted and grounded in the Scriptures that they never depart from them, ever directing themselves as well as their listeners to its truths. Biblical preaching should be just that—*biblical*." He continues, "But this biblical prescription is an unknown remedy for many preachers today. In their zeal to lead popular and successful ministries, many are becoming less concerned with pointing to the biblical text. Their use of the Bible is much like the singing of the national anthem before a ballgame—something merely heard at the beginning, but never referenced again, a necessary preliminary that becomes an awkward intrusion to the real event. In their attempt to be contemporary and relevant, many pastors talk *about* the Scriptures, but, sadly, they rarely speak *from* them."[23]

Unlike the listeners of Jesus' day, we are privileged to have God's Word (the seed) in written form. We should take advantage of that privilege and bring a copy of the Scriptures with us whenever we go to worship. This helps us recognize if the person proclaiming God's Word (sowing the seed) is speaking the truth.

Next Jesus explained the different kinds of soil. All four of these types of soil are depicted in people who hear God's Word. Some have hard-soil souls, some have rocky-soil souls, some have thorny-soil souls, and some have fertile-soil souls. Let's look at all four as we see Jesus' explanation unfold.

He started with the hard pathway:

> The seed that fell on the footpath represents those who hear the message, only to have Satan come at once and take it away.
>
> MARK 4:15

With this explanation, we immediately know what the first soil represents. It's the condition of the recipient's heart, the internal state of the soul. Remember what came and took the seed away? It was the birds. In this case, the birds in the story represent Satan. Jesus interpreted the parable, but as He told the story, He didn't say, "The devil comes and takes the seed." He gives them an analogy they can understand. His listeners had all seen birds fluttering around a farmer, hoping for a nice meal as he walked along sowing his seed. Now Jesus said, in effect, "This hard soil represents those with hard hearts."

You might attend church because that's the thing to do on Sunday. You listen to the sermon, and then you're out the door. You have no plans to allow God's truth to impact your life. After all, let's not get fanatical about this! So you drift through the empty motions of religion, but none of it grips you or reaches you deep within. What's wrong? You may have a hard heart. The seed lies there, and shortly thereafter it is taken away by the enemy. Believe me, the enemy doesn't want you to think about God's Word—ever! He wants to take away the seed immediately, leaving you empty and with nothing to fall back on. Then you go about living life on your own, maybe sinking into depression or just doing what you want because you think you don't need God. But that's not the journey the Lord would have us take. He wants us to hear His truth and let it sink in, to take root in our lives. The hard-hearted response is to shove God's Word aside—to procrastinate when it comes to studying it, and ultimately to ignore it.

CORRELATING THE PARABLE

Let's do some correlation right now. The Bible includes an example of someone with a hard heart—a man named Felix. We read about Felix, a governor, in Acts 24. In your notes, write, "Acts 24:22-27: Governor Felix."

The apostle Paul was a captive of Rome. Felix brought Paul before him and allowed him a hearing. Paul explained the gospel to Felix (he spread the seed). Felix wasn't ready to hear it, however, and he gave the order for Paul to be kept in custody (see Acts 24:23). Later, Felix brought Paul back, and after hearing a little more about Jesus, he got rid of Paul again. Felix is a classic example of someone with a hard heart. He listened to the message of God, but instead of taking it seriously, he played around with it. You have a hard heart if you continually surround yourself with spiritual truth yet keep putting off a commitment to follow Christ. The seed never takes root; God's Word never penetrates.

Another example of having a hard heart is Alexander the coppersmith, who is mentioned in 2 Timothy 4:14-15. In Paul's last letter, he says, "[This man] did me much harm. . . . He fought against everything we said." Alexander was a hard-hearted man who was uninterested in the gospel.

Next, Jesus mentioned the rocky soil:

> The seed on the rocky soil represents those who hear the message and immediately receive it with joy. But since they don't have deep roots, they don't last long. They fall away as soon as they have problems or are persecuted for believing God's word.
>
> MARK 4:16-17

Here Jesus is describing a person who is trying to find a shortcut to faith. I'm picturing someone emerging out of a sinful background, claiming conversion, tossing around a verse or two, running around with a few Christians, and hoping to become a "celebrity Christian" because of this person's dramatic turnaround. Everybody applauds the story, scintillating as it is, because this person "got religion" . . . that is, until the going gets tough. When that happens, hard times multiply. Maybe this person experiences some persecution, faces conflict with authority, has financial troubles, or lacks mentoring. Before long, disillusionment replaces zeal. Then what we have on our hands is a modern-day Judas.

It's helpful to remember that Judas heard all the teaching the other disciples heard. Judas was numbered among the disciples of Jesus, remember? Think about it! He was exposed to all the miracles; he heard all the messages; he saw all those incredible life-changing events. But the truth never really took root or bore fruit. He was spiritually lost. In fact, Jesus later referred to him as the "son of perdition" (John 17:12, kjv).

It would be a good idea to do a study about Judas as you correlate this passage. His rocky-soil soul became his undoing. He tolerated the gospel, but he never really embraced it or allowed it to take root.

Maybe this is your story too. You like being with other Christians, and you like the benefits they bring—a few business contacts, perhaps. Or maybe you like the peace you feel when you hear the songs at church, or you feel a little warm inside when you hear something the preacher says. You're drawn to some parts of church, but you're not truly a follower of Jesus. If that describes you, you may have a rocky-soil heart.

John records a sad scene with some followers like that:

> At this point many of his disciples turned away and deserted him.
> JOHN 6:66

No longer was Jesus feeding His followers' stomachs. He wasn't performing as many miracles. As a result, many decided they'd had enough. They were out of there. People like that are as lost as they can be, even though you might think they're saved because of their short-lived fervor when they first claimed to know Christ. But over the long haul, they demonstrate a lack of authenticity. No roots. No fruit. No faith. No life in Christ.

Now Jesus' story gets really interesting. The thorny soil is mentioned next. Pay close attention.

> The seed that fell among the thorns represents others who hear God's word, but all too quickly the message is crowded

out by the worries of this life, the lure of wealth, and the
desire for other things, so no fruit is produced.

MARK 4:18-19

Epithumia is the Greek word translated "desire." This could refer
to a wholesome desire or an unwholesome desire. In this case, it's
an evil desire. Along with life's worries and the powerful lure to get
rich, people with thorny-soil souls have an ever-growing desire for
"other things." They're caught up in materialism. The old bumper
sticker pretty much sums up this mind-set: "The one who dies
with the most toys wins." Is this what you believe when nobody's
looking? You're driven to get rich. There's nothing inherently
wrong with wealth, but there's something deceitful about the *love*
of riches. It can backfire on you!

Blake Proctor gives this example:

Dan, a single guy living at home with his father and working
in the family business, found out he was going to inherit a
fortune when his sickly father died. The son decided that
he'd need a wife with which to share his fortune.

One evening at an investment meeting he spotted the
most beautiful woman he had ever seen. Her natural beauty
took his breath. "I may look like just an ordinary man," he
said to her, "but in just a few years, my father will die, and I
will inherit $65 million."

Impressed, the woman obtained his business card. Three
days later, she became his stepmother.[24]

By the principles of Jesus' parable, this man had a thorny-soil
heart. His life was consumed by the lure of superficial things—a
desire that always deceives in the end. Or consider this story. When
one man proposed to a woman, he said, "Darling, darling, I want

you to know that I love you more than anything else in the world. I want you to marry me! We'd have a great life together. Now, I'm not rich. I don't have a yacht or a Rolls Royce like Johnny Brown, but I do love you with all my heart." She thought for a few moments and then replied, "And I love you with all my heart, too . . . but *tell me more about Johnny Brown!*"

The love of money crowds out the truth of Scripture. When the Bible talks to the thorny-soil soul about sacrifice, it's almost like an obscene word. Sacrifice speaks of giving up your will for the will of the Lord Jesus. The response in a thorny heart is, "Not yet!"

Would it help to have a biblical example of one who got lost in the thorny soil? In 2 Timothy 4:10 we meet Demas, the man who "[loved] the things of this life." Demas abandoned Paul. In Dr. Richard Seume's excellent book *Shoes for the Road*, he calls Demas's departure "the lure of a lesser loyalty."[25]

Thorny soil is well represented throughout the Bible. We're not able to tell whether the thorny-soil soul is saved or lost. Not wanting to make it "walk on all fours," I'm not going to make a dogmatic statement about that. If this description portrays you, you must ask yourself, *Is that because I don't know Christ or because I'm walking in the flesh and not the Spirit? Have I yielded to things that would lure me into a sinful habit, even an addiction? Am I saved?* Those are questions for you to answer.

Finally, there is the fertile soil mentioned at the end of the story.

And the seed that fell on good soil represents those who hear and accept God's word and produce a harvest of thirty, sixty, or even a hundred times as much as had been planted!

MARK 4:20

The word *accept* comes from the Greek term *dechomai*, which means "to welcome." The good-soil soul hears the truth and welcomes it. If that's you, then you crave the Word of God. You long for the good seed to be planted. You welcome its entrance into your life. You appreciate its exhortation and its encouragement. You love to come together with fellow believers around the Word of God, and you long to worship the living God. You're like the deer mentioned in that lovely worship chorus:

> As the deer panteth for the water
> so my soul longeth after Thee.

You're like Timothy in Acts 16. He heard and believed, and then he began to travel with Paul. You're like Nicodemus in John 3. He met with Jesus, longing to find out more about the second birth. By John 19, the seed had taken root in Nicodemus and he was making it known to the other Pharisees that he was a devoted follower of Jesus. He even helped prepare the body of the Savior for burial after He was crucified.

If you're like one of these genuine followers of Jesus, I applaud you for your ongoing commitment.

APPLYING THE PARABLE

Here's something interesting about this parable: all four soils *hear* the Word. Go back and look for yourself. The pathway soil heard the Word. The rocky soil heard the Word. The thorny soil heard the Word. And the fertile soil heard and welcomed the Word. When the seed is planted, all hear the truth. There's nothing wrong with their hearing; the problem is with their heeding. So many are "hard of listening" when it comes to the truth. There's nothing wrong with the seed; the problem is obviously with the soil.

As I bring this chapter to a close, I urge you to pause long enough to ask yourself, *Which soil am I?*

Here's the main message of the parable: the condition of your heart will determine the destiny of your life. When you stand before your Maker, He will not ask, "How many church services did you attend?" Or, "How much money did you give?" Or, "How hard did you work to prune those thorns from your life?" No. He will more likely ask, "What did you do with the seed that was delivered into your ears? Did it take root in your soul? Did it make any difference in the way you lived? Did it influence the way you responded to life's challenges? Did you submit yourself, first and foremost, to Christ and His Cross?" Those are crucial questions. Remember the main message: the condition of your heart will determine the destiny of your life.

Which soil represents your heart? Your spouse or your closest friend or your parent cannot answer that question for you. You must answer it for yourself. By the grace of God and His faithful patience, you can come to the place where you'll hear and welcome God's truth.

Before you can serve the truth to others, you must taste it for yourself. But this isn't always easy. Even when your heart represents the fertile soil of this parable, hearing and teaching God's Word can be challenging, especially when the place you're serving it is difficult. The following chapter addresses that very real challenge.

Just as it's important for a chef to sample the food before serving it to others, we need to apply God's Word to our own lives before teaching (or preaching) it to others. Right now I'd like to invite you to take some time to examine your own heart. This exercise will serve as an example for you to follow each time you study the Scriptures.

1. Read 1 Peter 1:13–2:3 slowly and thoughtfully, and observe the passage carefully. List the types of ungodly behaviors that Peter tells believers to rid themselves of. What does Peter describe as the imperishable seed of God? What does that seed allow us to do? Since we have tasted that the Lord is good, what nutrition does Peter suggest we are to crave, and why?

2. In chapter 7, we learned about Psalm 139 and how God created us. In that chapter, David details how God created us, knows us, and remains with us. In the final two verses of this psalm, David asks God to search his heart and convict him of any sin in his life. Find a quiet place where you won't be interrupted and carefully read through Psalm 139, meditating on how great God is and recording

several specific characteristics about Him that you are most grateful for.

Read the final two verses of Psalm 139 out loud, praying that God's Spirit will search your heart. Respond to the Spirit's prompting with confession, repentance, gratitude, and praise.

3. Read Isaiah 6:10-13. In this passage the prophet Isaiah is calling the people of Judah to surrender their self-reliance and submit to God. What are you to do (and not do) with your eyes, ears, and heart in order to respond in obedience to God's holy Word?

4. Read Psalm 19, which explains how God speaks through creation and His Word. Pay particular attention to verses 7-11, which describe the Scriptures. Write down the characteristics of God's Word. According to this passage, how can we be free of guilt and innocent of great sin before the Lord? Use Psalm 19:14 as the basis for an earnest prayer to God. Write this prayer in your own words, and use it to pray before your next teaching opportunity.

CHAPTER 10

FEEDING THE HUNGRY

Presenting the Truth

No matter where we live—whether we're in a suburban neighborhood with a church on every corner, a religiously diverse city, or a remote village that doesn't yet have the Word of God in the people's heart language—there are spiritually hungry people all around us. Everyone has a deeply wired longing to worship something greater than themselves, and if people don't know the one true God, they will seek to curb that craving with a lesser god—an idol. For some people, their idols are tangible objects they bow down to in a shrine or temple. For others, their objects of worship are less tangible, such as money or reputation or status, but they are no less destructive.

The Word of God is the only thing that will feed starving, otherwise-empty souls. The nourishment that we glean as we observe, interpret, correlate, and apply is not merely for ourselves. Our calling is to serve the hungry "the bread of life"—Jesus Himself (John 6:35).

Jesus and His eternal, gratifying truths are what people are starving for, even if they don't realize it.

A SCENE FROM ANCIENT ATHENS

In first-century Athens, the apostle Paul found himself in a city overtaken by idolatry. Paul was once Saul of Tarsus, a monotheistic, strict Pharisee. He had cut his teeth on the Decalogue, or Ten Commandments, learning first, "You shall have no other gods before Me" (Exodus 20:3, NKJV). Throughout his life and ministry, Paul repeatedly affirmed that God and God alone is worthy of worship. There is no other. In fact, to worship any other is to prostitute one's faith. After Paul's dramatic encounter with Christ, he saw Jesus as the fulfillment of all that the Old Testament points to.

On one occasion during his travels, Paul went to Athens, a cultural, intellectual setting where he found himself surrounded by idols—literally. The Greek scholars wrote about the many idols in the city in Paul's day. Pausanias says, "Athens had more images than all the rest of Greece put together." Pliny adds, "In the time of Nero, Athens had well over 25,000 to 30,000 public statues excluding 30,000 in the Parthenon." Petronius sneers, "Why, it's easier to find a god than a man in Athens."

Luke, who wrote the book of Acts, begins his descriptive account by stating:

> Now while Paul waited for them at Athens, his spirit was provoked within him when he saw that the city was given over to idols.
>
> ACTS 17:16, NKJV

Given where Paul found himself, it's no wonder that he was "provoked" in his spirit. The original Greek word, *paroxuno*, means "stirred up, irritated, provoked, exercised, stimulated, urged to action." Of course he was stirred up—there were idols everywhere! You've heard of *Sleepless in Seattle*; here we find Paul "aghast in Athens." Everywhere he looked, he saw idols. They were etched into monuments, set up inside buildings, chiseled out of stone, and crafted into every shape and size from every imaginable substance. Xenophon called Athens "one great altar, one great offering to the gods!"[26]

Paul wasn't angry; he was heartsick. He didn't feel hatred for the Athenians; instead, he was overwhelmed by sadness. He realized that these people were so starved for something or someone to worship that their finest artisans kept sculpting and erecting idols, hoping that this one would work, or maybe that one. They even had one statue called *Agnosto Theo*, or "Unknown God." In other words: "In case we missed one, we'll build this one that has no name and identify it 'Unknown One.'"

Paul could neither sit still nor keep silent. His inner turmoil had to be expressed somehow. As was his custom when visiting a city, Paul first found his way to the synagogue. There he spoke to Jews and to God-fearing Gentiles alike. But that wasn't enough, so he moved into what we would call the mall. Athenians called it the *agora*, the marketplace. There he stood and boldly proclaimed the God of heaven and earth and His Son, Jesus Christ, who had been crucified and had risen from the dead.

Soon the philosophers gathered, as they often did in the agora. It didn't take long for them to realize what kind of person they had among them. They had a slang word for him: a "seed picker." That's the same word they would use for a plagiarist. In their view, he'd picked up a little philosophy here and plucked a few lines from there, and then by throwing them together, he'd come up with an intriguing story about some God of heaven.

These philosophers realized there was one place Paul should go if he wanted to have intelligent dialogue about his teaching, so they escorted him to the Areopagus. This word means "Mars Hill." There he would have a real platform where he could speak his mind.

If you traveled to Athens today, you would likely visit the Parthenon. Across from the stately Parthenon, there is a solid granite deposit almost four hundred feet high. For decades, the sloping sides were slick from tourists trying to climb to the top. Finally a stairway was built, making the climb easier and safer. That massive rock is the same place Paul stood. Why there? Because that was where the Athenian supreme court met. It was there that they heard cases of homicide, dealt with issues of morality, settled unresolved conflicts and complicated legal matters, and handled whatever else was brought before them.

Paul was escorted to this place where the prestigious minds of Athens, called Areopagites, gathered. There's debate as to how many Areopagites there were—maybe as few as twelve, perhaps as many as thirty. It may be that others from the general public were allowed to stand around the edges and listen. Imagine how Paul must have felt as he stood among them as the lone Christian. It must have been one of those moments in his life when he thought, *For this I was born.*

Think about it: this was a window of opportunity opened by the providence of God—one that would never reopen for Paul. As the eggheads of Athens met with the "seed picker" from Jerusalem, they must have wondered what he had to say that could possibly hold their attention. Talk about a tough place to deliver a speech. But Paul was neither intimidated nor reluctant. He didn't stutter. He stepped up, stood tall, and set forth an intriguing message. It was brief but powerful.

As we dive into Acts 17:22, remember what we've learned about observation: *What does the Bible say?* And then there's interpretation: *What does it mean?* Our study is embellished with correlation: *What does the Bible say elsewhere on the same or similar subjects?* The crowning step is application: *What does this passage say to me or to someone else?* Let's walk through all four steps as we examine Paul's presentation.

You'll notice that the quotation marks in your Bible begin in verse 22 and end at verse 31, where Paul refers to the resurrection of Jesus. He may have said more, but Luke records only these words. Let's work our way through them, being careful not to miss anything important. Don't allow your mind to wander.

> So Paul, standing before the council, addressed them as follows: "Men of Athens, I notice that you are very religious in every way."
>
> ACTS 17:22

The first thing we notice is that Paul's speech is recorded in only ten verses. To ensure that you don't overlook anything significant, I recommend reading this speech several times, both silently and aloud. I timed it and learned that Paul's message took about two minutes to deliver. Amazing. Paul was succinct and to the point, "a master of condensation," as Charles Spurgeon, the nineteenth-century British preacher, once described him.

We can also observe that Paul used terms anyone could understand. That's important to remember, since one of the characteristics of a good speech is that nobody gets turned off or bypassed because of the verbiage. He didn't use "Christianese," because his listeners weren't Christians. He didn't mention his theological training at the feet of Gamaliel, because that would have meant little to them; they were philosophers, not theologians. His language would be of interest to and understood by the general public, both young and old alike. There was no "secret code" people needed to know to understand Paul's message.

Let me mention another observation. Paul delivered his message without any time to prepare. The Athenians took him from the mall directly to Mars Hill, where he stepped up and delivered his speech. He held no scroll of the Scriptures. There was no quiet place to gather his thoughts or put together his speech. But we can be sure he had a reservoir of truth deep within his heart. His spontaneous speech emerged from his years of study. When he opened his mouth, his words made sense.

Not only were his words biblically sound, but they also connected with his listeners. It's not enough to just know Scripture; we also need to be able to build bridges to our audience. It's easy to think we're being understood when that isn't actually the case.

Let me give you a humorous example. Bubba had shingles. When he walked into the doctor's office, the receptionist asked him what he had. Bubba said simply, "Shingles." So she wrote down his name, address, and insurance number, and told him to have a seat.

Fifteen minutes later, a nurse came out and again asked Bubba what he had. He simply said, "Shingles." She wrote down his height, his weight, and a complete medical history, and told him to wait in the examining room.

Half an hour later, a nurse came in and asked Bubba what he had. "Shingles," he said again. So the nurse gave Bubba a blood test, a blood pressure test, and an electrocardiogram. She then told Bubba to take off all his clothes and wait for the doctor.

An hour later the doctor came in and found Bubba sitting patiently in the nude. He asked Bubba what he had. "Shingles!"

"Where?" the doctor asked.

"Outside on the truck," Bubba said. "Where do you want me to unload them?"

Sometimes you think you're communicating clearly when, in fact, you've completely missed the mark!

Paul didn't miss the mark on Mars Hill. He was building a bridge with his audience—a bridge built with words. His words took his listeners from where they were to where he wanted them to go. His plan was to introduce them to someone they'd never met.

PAUL'S SPEAKING TECHNIQUES

As I've thought through Paul's speech, I've discovered five techniques Paul used that we can employ today.

First, Paul started where his listeners were. "Men of Athens, I notice that you are very religious in every way" (Acts 17:22). Let's pause for a moment, leaving Paul standing alongside these philosophers, and picture the scene. He doesn't insult his audience; he doesn't condemn them. Instead, he begins with a rather gracious opening line: "I notice that you men are very religious." When feeding the hungry, it helps to create an appetite.

In his book *Vanishing Grace*, Philip Yancey writes,

It makes a huge difference whether I treat a nonbeliever as someone who is *wrong* rather than as someone who is on the way but lost. For a helpful model I look to the apostle Paul's speech in the cultural center of Athens, as recorded in Acts 17. Instead of condemning his audience to hell for practicing idolatry, Paul begins by commending their spiritual search, especially their devotion to an "unknown God." God planned creation and human life, Paul told the Athenians, so that "we would seek him and perhaps reach out for him and find him, though he is not far from any one of us." He builds his case from common ground, quoting two of their own writers to affirm basic truths. Demonstrating a humble respect for his audience, Paul circles the themes of lostness and estranged family before presenting a richer understanding of a God who cannot be captured in images of gold, silver, or stone.[27]

Had you been one of the sophisticated Areopagites, you would not have felt put off or put down by his opening line. He started where they were, and his statement grabbed their attention. Then he continued:

> For as I was walking along I saw your many shrines. And one of your altars had this inscription on it: "To an Unknown God." This God, whom you worship without knowing, is the one I'm telling you about.
>
> ACTS 17:23

The philosophers lived in Athens, and most of them had likely been there all their adult lives, some since they were children. They had walked among the shrines, and they knew exactly what Paul was talking about. He established common ground with his listeners right from the start.

Evangelist Billy Graham was gifted at connecting with his audience too. He would arrive at a city before his crusade began and make a study of the area. Then when he stood before the people, he would refer to some of the unique features of their city at the beginning of his message. It's an excellent principle to remember: begin where the audience is.

Notice, however, that Paul didn't flatter his audience. "I notice that you are very religious." That was a true statement. Having stood in the midst of the shrines—tens of thousands of them— Paul remembered one: *Agnosto Theo*. While standing among these intelligent men, he called to mind that particular idol and said, in effect, "I saw this 'Unknown God,' this God whom you worship without knowing. You don't know Him, but I've met Him and I'm here to introduce you to Him."

I don't know about you, but when I was reading this account for the umpteenth time, I smiled, realizing the genius of this segue from an idol to the living Lord. Paul built a bridge with words to capture his audience's attention. He started where they were.

Second, Paul used the familiar to introduce the unfamiliar. We saw this principle played out in the last chapter, when Jesus told the parable of the sower. We read about the hard soil, the shallow soil, the thorny soil, and the fertile soil. We also noted how appropriate it was for Jesus to choose an illustration from agriculture since it was familiar to all his listeners. In this case, Paul pointed to an "Unknown God" and said, in effect, "This God is unknown to you right now, but He's not only knowable; He's available. Let me tell you about Him." What an excellent transition!

Third, Paul developed his theme clearly and logically. Observe the bridge that Paul continued to build with his words:

> He is the God who made the world and everything in it. Since he is Lord of heaven and earth, he doesn't live in manmade temples, and human hands can't serve his needs— for he has no needs. He himself gives life and breath to everything, and he satisfies every need.
>
> ACTS 17:24-25

The fact that God made the world and everything in it was news to these philosophers. They'd been taught by the brightest minds in Athens and beyond, but they'd never been taught about the Creator God.

If you traveled to Greece today and hired a local guide, you'd learn all about the mythology of Greece but nothing about the God of heaven. Religion is dripping with mythology, just as Athens was surrounded by numerous gods. So Paul boldly announced that he would tell them about "the God who made the world and everything in it." Can you imagine how puzzled those philosophers must have been when Paul introduced them to the "Lord of heaven and earth"? Note the change from God to Lord. This is not just the God who created all things in heaven and on earth; He's the *Lord* of heaven and earth.

Stop and think about the way God is being described here. As the Creator, He cannot be contained. As the Originator, He has no needs. Since He is intelligent, He has a definite plan. In fact, He satisfies every need. Paul was on a roll; he didn't hold back.

> From one man he created all the nations throughout the whole earth. He decided beforehand when they should rise and fall, and he determined their boundaries.
>
> ACTS 17:26

Who's the one man? It's Adam, of course. However, those Athenian philosophers had never heard that story. It's found in Genesis, a scroll not found in their library. Paul never once quoted a verse from the Old Testament, nor did he speak the name of Christ. Remember—his audience was unfamiliar with the biblical story. Instead, he mentioned the One who began with "one man" through whom God "created all the nations throughout the whole earth."

As if that weren't enough, notice Paul's veiled reference to God's sovereignty over the nations. *They* in this verse refers to the nations. The nations haven't simply emerged out of an evolutionary past. The continents didn't form simply as a result of massive geological changes. No, the nations have been determined by the God of heaven. He knows exactly what He's doing. He has a divinely devised plan, and it's unfolding exactly as the Creator God arranged it.

Paul made the point that although the people may never have heard the Lord's voice and although there's no physical image of Him, He has arranged the world according to His plan.

So where did Paul go from there in his speech? He had the last few "word bricks" to lay in his bridge. Having used the familiar to introduce the unfamiliar, he developed his theme clearly and logically. At this point they were probably thinking, *This is getting pretty deep.* Their minds may have started to wander. That's when he stepped in with another technique.

Fourth, he used interesting illustrations to hold their attention.

His purpose was for the nations to seek after God and perhaps feel their way toward him and find him—though he is not far from any one of us.

ACTS 17:27

It's worth noting that Paul quoted from Aratus of Soli (a passage he had obviously memorized, not having had time to prepare his speech). In his education, Paul had no doubt studied Aratus, who lived in third century BC. He wisely quoted only one line of the poem. Let me give you the first three lines, and you'll understand why Paul omitted those lines:

Zeus fills the streets, the marts;
    Zeus fills the seas, the shores, the rivers!
Everywhere our need is Zeus!
    We also are his offspring.

Paul didn't mention Zeus, because although the Athenians may have believed that Zeus was the zenith god, he isn't the God of heaven and earth. Paul was simply saying, "The one I'm introducing to you is the One who truly is our Father, the Father of all people." Continue reading his speech as it unfolds:

For in him we live and move and exist. As some of your own poets have said, "We are his offspring." And since this is true, we shouldn't think of God as an idol designed by craftsmen from gold or silver or stone.

ACTS 17:28-29

The bridge is just about finished. But the Athenians were still scratching their heads and pulling their beards wondering, *Where is he going with this?* This is when Paul employs his final technique.

Fifth, Paul applies the message personally and effectively. Let's take a look:

> God overlooked people's ignorance about these things in earlier times, but now he commands everyone everywhere to repent of their sins and turn to him. For he has set a day for judging the world with justice by the man he has appointed, and he proved to everyone who this is by raising him from the dead.
>
> ACTS 17:30-31

The word *repent* is one of those key words we need to check out. It means "to change one's mind." It captures the idea of going in one direction and then turning to head in the opposite direction. In relation to sin, this means a complete turnaround. We know the One whom God raised from the dead, but the philosophers didn't.

With Paul's statement about the Resurrection, the people stopped listening. But don't think for a moment that they missed the point. And don't think that Paul was unaware of the fact that the Athenians were taught from childhood that there was no resurrection. They cut their educational teeth on words like this quote, which is attributed to the god Apollo in *The Eumenides*: "Once a man dies and the earth drinks up his blood, there is no resurrection." When they realized where Paul was going, their defenses went up. To cross this bridge meant trusting in someone besides themselves, turning to the One who had died for their sins and had been raised from the dead.

Just as quickly as the dialogue began, the brakes began to screech. Some of Paul's listeners started to laugh. Let's observe three common reactions to Jesus' resurrection, beginning at verse 32.

> When they heard Paul speak about the resurrection of the dead, some laughed in contempt, but others said, "We want to hear more about this later." That ended Paul's discussion with them, but some joined him and became believers.
>
> ACTS 17:32-34

The response of most of the audience was along these lines: "Are you kidding me? You believe that nonsense?" Interestingly, Paul didn't plead with them or beg them to believe. He didn't even call for a response. Notice that while some scoffed, others responded, "We want to hear more about this later." (One of the most dangerous words a person could ever use after hearing the gospel is *later*.)

DO NOT WAIT FOR "LATER"

Recently a forty-eight-year-old man said to me, "I was a specimen of health, and not long ago, I got a headache. It was kind of strong. The person I was with said, 'Can I give you an aspirin?' I said, 'No, I'll be okay.' But soon I was vomiting and fighting diarrhea, and then I fainted. The next thing I knew, I woke up in a hospital. I'd had a stroke." Forty-eight years old. The doctor told him after the examination, "You should have died three separate times, but amazingly you're alive." When I asked my friend for permission to use his story, he said, "Please do—it may awaken people not to procrastinate."

My friend told me he was ready to die because he had already trusted Christ. If you haven't done so yet, you may think you have plenty of time. You think you can call the shots and accept Christ later. You say, "Perhaps I'll become a Christian after the beginning of the year or when I get the job I'm looking for." Or, "Perhaps I'll make the commitment when I get past this battle with drugs or alcohol. After I conquer that, I'll be able to move in the right direction." Don't be fooled! Those who say "later" often die with the word on their lips. You don't know when there will be a car collision or when your heart will beat for the last time. I'm told by my physician that when many heart attacks occur, there is no pain whatsoever; the person simply dies.

If you have never trusted in the Lord Jesus Christ, learn a lesson from those who foolishly said, "We'll talk to him later." (By the way, there's no record in Acts or elsewhere in the Scriptures that those who procrastinated ever came back to talk to Paul.)

I am impressed, however, with the fact that there were a few in Athens who believed soon after Paul's message. Look at this:

> But some joined him and became believers. Among them were Dionysius, a member of the council, a woman named Damaris, and others with them.
>
> ACTS 17:34

Talk about believing under pressure! One of the Athenians, Dionysius, said, in essence, "I've crossed this bridge. I want to know more about the One who died and was raised for me." Then there was a believer named Damaris. We know nothing more of this woman except that she's named here. And don't think that was the extent of the converts. Please observe that "some joined him and became believers." There were others beyond just these two who are named, but we don't know how many. We don't know anything about their backgrounds; all we know is that somehow Paul was able to apply the message in such a way that they couldn't miss it or turn it off.

In the previous chapter, I asked you to find yourself in the parable about the types of soil. At the end of this chapter, I ask you to find yourself on Mars Hill. Are you among those who walk away and sneer as you say, "Oh, how could anyone believe something like this?" You have the freedom to do that. You can choose to reject the message of forgiveness and eternal hope. Or you may tragically think that, by putting off the decision, you're not turning it off entirely. But in fact you are, because you're counting on later when that's not guaranteed at all. Or maybe you're among those of us who, by the grace of God, have decided that the One who died for us is worth everything, and we trust Him.

There is urgency when it comes to feeding the Scriptures to the hungry. The food must be carefully planned and well prepared. Like Paul, you may one day be called to feed people on the spot. Not everyone will appreciate the meal; some will walk away hungry. The account in Acts 17 proves that. But when Scripture is properly studied and taught, God's Spirit will move and draw those whose hearts are hungry for the Bread of Life. Our goal is to prepare it well and serve it in the most appealing way possible. When we do, the hungry will be fed . . . and God will be glorified.

Feeding the hungry isn't always easy. As we saw with Paul on Mars Hill, sometimes God's Word is met with resistance. However, our call is to carefully, graciously, and boldly present the truths of Scripture, regardless of how others respond. This exercise will challenge you to try this for yourself.

1. Find an opportunity to present a passage of Scripture and its meaning to someone else. This might be an opportunity that comes through your church or over coffee with a friend. Whether you're teaching to one person or a small group, take time to prepare carefully. This includes knowing a little about your audience to create a bridge from their life experiences to the biblical truths you will present. Follow the model of *observation, interpretation, correlation,* and *application.* You may want to present one of the passages we've discussed in this book or one of the passages from a previous exercise.

2. Carefully consider your audience and how best to help them apply the passage. Pray for the Spirit's guidance as you prepare. Then, like the apostle Paul on Mars Hill, present the truths of Scripture and trust that God will

use His Word for His glory. Remember what we learned from Paul's speaking techniques as you consider the following:

Remember the spiritual maturity level of your listeners— whether they're mature believers, new Christians, or maybe even people who have never heard the truths of God's Word.

Use the familiar to introduce the unfamiliar. What everyday examples can your audience relate to that will help them understand the Scriptures?

Develop your theme clearly and logically. Carefully explain the connection between the illustration you use and the truth of the biblical passage.

Use interesting illustrations to hold your audience's attention. Tie the truths of God's Word directly to your listeners so they feel the impact on their own lives.

Apply the message personally and effectively. Present the truth with a call to action, encouraging your listeners to respond.

After your teaching session, record the results. Were you pleased with the way the presentation went? If you had the opportunity to do this again with the same people, what changes would you make the second time around? Be assured that the more you are engaged in presenting God's Word, the more comfortable you will be.

A FINAL WORD

BON APPÉTIT

Providing Nourishing Meals for Yourself and Others

DURING OUR MORE THAN SIXTY YEARS of marriage, Cynthia and
I have had the pleasure of enjoying a number of delectable meals
together. To this day, several stand out as those among the best.

We will never forget the five-course candlelight dinner we ate
overlooking Kapalua Bay on Maui as we celebrated our twenty-
fifth anniversary. With a full moon overhead, flaming tiki torches
surrounding us, and the distant silhouette of Molokai across the
horizon of the blue Pacific, the lovely atmosphere enhanced our
delicious meal. What a memorable, romantic evening!

While on an international trip with my sister and several
friends, we ate at the historic Ritz hotel in Paris. We had a grand
time together—and what a sumptuous dinner we were served!
From the moment we entered the dining room until we got up to
leave, we were enveloped in elegance.

After two Insight for Living rallies with thousands of faithful
listeners in Memphis, Tennessee, our leadership team slipped away
to enjoy those famous dry-rubbed barbecued ribs with all the delicious trimmings in a basement restaurant called Charlie Vergo's
Rendezvous. Talk about fabulous taste and equally great atmosphere! Lively bluegrass music in the background added the perfect

touch. My older son dared me to try to outeat him. I don't remember who won, but I stopped at twelve thick ribs!

Back in the mid-1960s, when I was serving as pastor of a little church in Waltham, Massachusetts, Cynthia and I rode with another couple halfway across the state to a quaint restaurant called the Old Mill, located deep in the woods not far from a quiet village. The ambience was as appealing as the delicious meals they served on pewter plates . . . and we're still wearing their desserts, especially their to-die-for crème brûlée.

Going back even further, when I was a Dallas Theological Seminary student and before we started our family, Cynthia and I designated every Friday night as our date night. Our favorite place to go was a hole-in-the-wall joint called Heath's Steakhouse in the Oak Lawn district. All the blue-collar customers sat on barstools at a counter and watched the cook broil their steaks. The waitress (who had a tattoo before tattoos were cool) had a face like three miles of bad road and called every man "hon" or "dahlin." We're talking a *seasoned* server! Don't laugh—the place fit our budget. The waitress could whip up a mixed garden salad in a plastic bowl and smother it with dressing faster than you could sneeze. Their piping-hot, medium-rare steak with a huge baked potato stuffed with butter, bacon, sour cream, and chives was absolutely out of this world. As we left, I always thought, *That was some kind of meal for eight bucks!*

And I dare not forget the Thanksgiving meals Cynthia and I prepared over the years with all our family members gathered around us. It was always our pleasure to fix and serve the traditional turkey and dressing as well as all the other yummy side dishes that accompany such feasts. And of course there were our three favorite pies, which Cynthia always prepared from scratch: pumpkin, lemon, and pecan. My mouth salivates just thinking about those meals we ate as we celebrated my favorite holiday of the year. Following the feast, we always stayed seated at the table as a family, sharing about what the year had included and especially what the Lord had taught us in the process . . . true stories often told with tears. You can't beat memories like that.

What is true of great meals is true of great messages that have been carefully prepared and attractively presented. Not only are they enlightening and enriching; they also feed our souls, and over time, they transform our lives.

As I reflect on the decades I've been a follower of Christ, I can vividly remember hearing a number of well-prepared, soul-satisfying messages that contributed to my spiritual growth. Invariably, they represented keen observations drawn from the Word of God and insightful, accurate interpretations that opened my heart to truths I would have missed on my own. As the verse or the passage of Scripture was correlated with other biblical passages, my understanding expanded. And when the application was appropriately set forth and driven home, exposing and invading areas of my life that needed to be corrected, I found nourishment and encouragement. How eminently blessed I've been to be the recipient of such healthy and wholesome instruction from gifted preachers and teachers throughout my life!

My main desire in writing this book has been to pass the baton in this all-important relay of the truth. I've written with the purpose of helping you know how to search the Scriptures on your own. Once you've mastered that skill, I want to stimulate you to pass the baton to others so that they, too, will learn to find precious treasures in God's Word and have their lives transformed. Then they can pass those truths on to others as well.

As you now understand, this divine relay never ends. In the spiritually starved world we live in, we must continue to serve spiritual meals to hungry people who desperately need nourishment. It is both our privilege and our responsibility to do so.

May your journey through the Bible never end. May your walk with Christ continue to deepen. May your knowledge and discernment increase as you humble yourself under the mighty hand of God. May you be used to encourage many to realize the feast that awaits them as they discover how to find the ingredients, prepare the food, and serve the meal that will, by God's grace and power, transform lives all around the world. Bon appétit!

ABOUT THE AUTHOR

CHARLES R. SWINDOLL has devoted his life to the accurate, practical teaching and application of God's Word and His grace. A pastor at heart, Chuck has served as a senior pastor to congregations in Texas, Massachusetts, and California. Since 1998, he has served as the founder and senior pastor-teacher of Stonebriar Community Church in Frisco, Texas, but Chuck's listening audience extends far beyond a local church body. A leading program in Christian broadcasting since 1979, *Insight for Living* airs in major Christian radio markets around the world, reaching people groups in languages they can understand. Chuck's extensive writing ministry has also served the body of Christ worldwide, and his leadership as president and now chancellor of Dallas Theological Seminary has helped prepare and equip a new generation of men and women for ministry. Chuck and his wife, Cynthia, his partner in life and ministry, have four grown children, ten grandchildren, and six great-grandchildren.

NOTES

1. A. W. Tozer, *God's Pursuit of Man* (Chicago: Moody, 2015), 20.

2. Robert Ballard, "A Long Last Look at Titanic," *National Geographic* (December 1986).

3. C. S. Lewis, *The Weight of Glory* (New York: HarperCollins, 2001), 58.

4. Charles H. Spurgeon, *The Golden Alphabet* (1887), preface.

5. C. S. Lewis, *The Problem of Pain*, in *The Complete C. S. Lewis Signature Classics* (New York: HarperCollins, 2006), 605.

6. William Tyndale, *Tyndale's Old Testament: Being the Pentateuch of 1530, Joshua to 2 Chronicles of 1537, and Jonah* (Yale University Press, 1992), 4.

7. Charles R. Swindoll, *Come before Winter* (Portland, OR: Multnomah, 1985), 120.

8. Bernard Ramm, *Protestant Biblical Interpretation: A Textbook of Hermeneutics* (Grand Rapids, MI: Baker, 1970), 4–5.

9. Ibid., 6.

10. John R. W. Stott, *Between Two Worlds* (Grand Rapids, MI: Eerdmans, 1982), 211.

11. Stephen Arterburn and Jack Felton, *Toxic Faith: Experiencing Healing from Painful Spiritual Abuse* (Colorado Springs: Waterbrook, 2001), 1–3.

12. Howard G. Hendricks and William D. Hendricks, *Living by the Book: The Art and Science of Reading the Bible* (Chicago: Moody, 1993), 231.

13. Walter Bauer, *A Greek-English Lexicon of the New Testament and Other Early Christian Literature*, ed. Frederick William Danker, 3rd ed. (Chicago: University of Chicago Press, 2001), 948.

14. William Barclay, *The Letters of James and Peter: The New Daily Study Bible* (Louisville, KY: Westminster John Knox Press, 2003), 402.

15. Ibid., 403.

16. A. W. Tozer, *The Root of the Righteous* (Chicago: Moody, 2015), 165.

17. Ryan Holiday, *The Obstacle Is the Way: The Timeless Art of Turning Trials into Triumph* (New York: Penguin, 2014), 66–67.

18. Roy B. Zuck, *The Speaker's Quote Book* (Grand Rapids, MI: Kregel, 2005), 309.

19. Ibid.

20. A. W. Tozer, *God's Pursuit of Man* (Chicago: Moody, 2015), 19.

21. James R. Edwards, *The Gospel according to Mark* (Grand Rapids, MI: Eerdmans, 2002), 126.

22. Warren Wiersbe, *Preaching and Teaching with Imagination: The Quest for Biblical Ministry* (Grand Rapids, MI: Baker, 2007), 52.

23. Steven J. Lawson, *Famine in the Land: A Passionate Call for Expository Preaching* (Chicago: Moody, 2003), 81–82.

24. Blake Proctor, "Financial Planning," Opinion, *Miller County Liberal*, November 30, 2011, http://www.millercountyliberal.com/news/2011-11-30/Opinion/Financial_planning.html.

25. Richard H. Seume, *Shoes for the Road* (Chicago: Moody, 1974), 29.

26. Edwin Wilbur Rice, *Commentary on the Acts* (Philadelphia: American Sunday-School Union, 1900), 224.

27. Philip Yancey, *Vanishing Grace: What Ever Happened to the Good News?* (Grand Rapids, MI: Zondervan, 2014), 11–12.

ALSO AVAILABLE
from
TYNDALE HOUSE PUBLISHERS
AND PASTOR CHUCK SWINDOLL

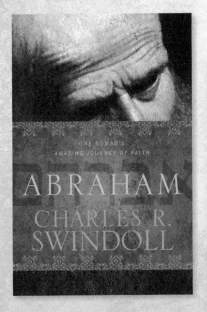

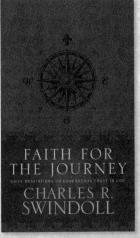

SAMPLE THE
FIRST CHAPTER OF
Abraham NOW.

GOING . . . NOT KNOWING

IN THE BEGINNING, God created everything—the universe, our
sun, this planet—and He populated the earth with plants, fish,
birds, animals, and finally humans. And it was good . . . in fact,
very good. Everything in creation existed in symbiotic collaboration
with everything else. That is, until Adam and his wife, Eve, the first
humans, violated their Creator's one and only rule: of all the millions
of fruit trees on the earth, do not eat the fruit of one specific tree
(see Genesis 2:15-17). When they chose to eat of that tree anyway,
despite the Creator's grave warning, everything changed. *Everything.*

Their choice to disobey God was an act of rebellion. They chose
to follow their own desires instead of trusting in God's leadership.
And their act of rebellion changed how the world operates. Before the
Fall, everything had worked according to God's grace, but after that
moment, the world quickly became a place characterized by suffering,
disease, pain, selfishness, violence, and death. People were born with
Adam's rebellious nature, and within just a few generations, the entire
human race became so incorrigibly corrupt that God wiped out all
but a handful of lives—Noah and his family (see Genesis 6–9).

Several generations after this new beginning, the human popu-
lation rebounded, but its moral condition was hardly any better.

In fact, by the time of Abraham, humanity was well on its way to becoming incorrigible again. People lived according to their own rules, which according to archaeological data included all kinds of vice and perversion. Instead of seeking to know God, their Creator, they exchanged truth for superstition. They entertained themselves with campfire stories of mythical spirit beings whose activities affected the physical world, they carved idols to represent these imaginary gods, and they then did appalling things to appease them.

God could have turned His back on creation. He could have abandoned humanity to its own self-destructive ignorance. He was not morally compelled to rescue humanity from the evil it created and perpetuated. Even so, God established a plan to redeem the world, beginning with one man. He would make this man a model recipient of saving grace and establish him as the founding father of a new and unique nation. In time, as the plan unfolded, this nation would become the means by which all the world might hear of the one true Creator God and return to Him.

God's redemptive plan began with His choice of a man named Abram.

GOD'S CHOSEN MAN

We know this man by the name Abraham, but he was born Abram. God changed his name at a critical point in the narrative, but for the first 99 of his 175 years, he answered to Abram.

He lived around the end of the Early Bronze Age (circa 2000 BC) in a thriving, bustling, cultured city known as "Ur of the Chaldeans" (Genesis 11:28). The land of the Chaldeans—also known as Mesopotamia—was located in present-day Iraq, which archaeologists and historians call the cradle of civilization because this is where ancient people first gathered into cities and established societies. "Few periods from ancient history are as well documented by artifacts and inscriptions as is the time of Abraham."

Consequently, we know a lot about this man's culture, religion, beliefs, and everyday life.

Abram was an ordinary member of his society, no different from his neighbors. Upon his birth, he received a name that means "the father is exalted"—most likely a reference to the deity worshiped by his family. People in ancient Mesopotamia worshiped a pantheon of mythical gods, ruled by the moon god, Sin, whom they regarded as "the lord of heaven" and "the divine creator." Like his relatives and neighbors, Abram worshiped idols and accepted mythology as truth (see Joshua 24:2). Even so, God appeared specifically to Abram and gave him personalized instructions: "Leave your native country, your relatives, and your father's family, and go to the land that I will show you" (Genesis 12:1).

It is important to note that God didn't appear to a group of people and then offer a general invitation to follow. We should also observe that Abram didn't seek out God for a relationship; God approached him. It's doubtful Abram had even heard of the one true Creator God before that point. By an act of pure grace, God dipped His hand into that idolatrous hole to select Abram out of all people.

Why this particular man? Did Abram turn from the idols of his ancestors and seek God? Did he make himself worthy of divine mercy? Far from it! The Lord chose Abram for reasons known only in heaven. We can say for certain that Abram did nothing to earn or deserve God's favor. Nevertheless, the Lord appeared to this ignorant, sinful, superstitious idol worshiper and said, "Leave your native country, your relatives, and your father's family, and go to the land that I will show you. I will make you into a great nation. I will bless you and make you famous, and you will be a blessing to others. I will bless those who bless you

The Lord chose Abram for reasons known only in heaven. Abram did nothing to earn or deserve God's favor.

and curse those who treat you with contempt. All the families on earth will be blessed through you" (Genesis 12:1-3).

God's call of Abram began with an imperative—a clear command. God told him to leave his country for a land that He would show him . . . sometime later. To receive the promised blessings, Abram had to leave behind everything he relied on for safety and provision—homeland and relatives—and trust that God would honor His commitment. A New Testament writer reflected on his ancestor, stating, "It was by faith that Abraham obeyed when God called him to leave home and go to another land that God would give him as his inheritance. He went without knowing where he was going" (Hebrews 11:8).

Stop and think about that for a moment. Put yourself in Abram's place. You're roughly seventy-five years old, with a wife in her midsixties. You've lived in one place your whole life. You have an established homestead in a familiar city with family and a community you've known since birth. Suddenly, the Lord appears to you in a physical manifestation—whether visual or auditory—you cannot deny as authentically supernatural, and He tells you to pack up and hit the road for an undisclosed destination. Can you imagine Abram's conversations with friends and neighbors?

"Oh, I see you're packing up, Abram."

"Yeah."

"Really? You're leaving town?"

"Yes, we leave in a few days."

"You know, you're not getting any younger. Are you ready to start all over somewhere?"

"Yep, Sarai and I are moving."

"Really? So, where are you going?"

"I don't know."

"You're packing up everything you have, leaving everything

familiar, and you have no idea where you're headed? Have you lost your mind?"

Everything within us recoils from making big changes without thorough planning. Most of us need to see where we're jumping before committing to a leap. But God called Abram to obey this call without complete information. Abram didn't know where he was going, so he couldn't trust in a well-thought-out, long-range plan. Nevertheless, the Lord gave Abram *sufficient* information to make a reasonable decision.

When Abram encountered the Lord, he knew that God was real. The awesome splendor of God's presence left him no room for doubt. Moreover, the Lord gave him three specific promises that made obedience worth his trouble. While his neighbors thought he had lost his mind, Abram had good reason to trust in God, even without knowing every detail of the plan.

GOD'S UNCONDITIONAL COVENANT

Different kinds of covenants appear throughout the Old Testament—some between individuals, others between nations. There are also several divine covenants, which are contracts or agreements between God and people. In the Garden of Eden, the Creator established a covenant with Adam and Eve: "You may freely eat the fruit of every tree in the garden—except the tree of the knowledge of good and evil" (Genesis 2:16-17). Note the promise: "If you eat its fruit, you are sure to die" (verse 17).

A little further in the Scriptures we come to Noah's time, when God said, "I have decided to destroy all living creatures, for they have filled the earth with violence. Yes, I will wipe them all out along with the earth! Build a large boat" (Genesis 6:13-14). When the floodwaters receded, the Lord promised, "I am con-firming my covenant with you. Never again will floodwaters kill all living creatures; never again will a flood destroy the earth. . . .

I am giving you a sign of my covenant with you and with all living creatures, for all generations to come. I have placed my rainbow in the clouds. It is the sign of my covenant with you and with all the earth" (Genesis 9:11-13).

Some covenants are conditional, meaning that fulfillment by one party depends upon fulfillment by the other. These agreements usually include if/then statements: "If you do your part, then I will do my part." When God settled the Israelites in the Promised Land, He established a conditional covenant with them: "If you fully obey the LORD your God and carefully keep all his commands that I am giving you today, the LORD your God will set you high above all the nations of the world. You will experience all these blessings if you obey the LORD your God" (Deuteronomy 28:1-2). Conversely, He said, "But if you refuse to listen to the LORD your God and do not obey all the commands and decrees I am giving you today, all these curses will come and overwhelm you. . . . The LORD himself will send on you curses, confusion, and frustration in everything you do, until at last you are completely destroyed for doing evil and abandoning me" (Deuteronomy 28:15, 20).

An unconditional covenant is a straightforward promise that contains no stipulations. In the Lord's first encounter with Abram, He established an unconditional covenant. He did give the patriarch a command, and Abram had to obey to claim the Lord's blessings. Still, the promises did not contain if/then statements. They were simple declarations:

> - "*I will* make you into a great nation" (Genesis 12:2).
> - "*I will* bless you and make you famous" (verse 2).
> - "*I will* bless those who bless you and curse those who treat you with contempt" (verse 3).
> - "All the families on earth *will be* blessed through you" (verse 3).

Note also that the covenant includes three major areas of blessing:

> a *national* blessing
> a *personal* blessing
> an *international* blessing

God promised a *national* unconditional blessing. Abram's descendants would be numerous enough to form a large nation. Let us not overlook the fact that God made this pledge to a man in his midseventies! Abram's wife, by then in her midsixties, had not given birth to any children. As a barren couple well past their prime, they had given up hope of having a single child, to say nothing of a whole nation of descendants. Yet the Lord promised, "I will make you into a great nation."

Today we know that God had in mind the nation of Israel, as history tells us that Abraham is the father of the Hebrew people. God made this promise to bless a nation without conditions; He guaranteed its fulfillment without fail. Of course, Abram and Sarai had to wait. They were not yet ready to receive this particular blessing. A twenty-five-year, faith-building journey lay before them. And when Abram's confidence wavered during those years between the promise and the fulfillment, the Lord reaffirmed His unconditional covenant at least two more times.

When Abram arrived in Canaan, the territory was overrun by the kind of evil that had precipitated the great Flood (see Genesis 6–9). To make matters worse, Abram relinquished part of his land claim to settle a family dispute (see Genesis 13:1-12). The Lord said to Abram, "Look as far as you can see in every direction—north and south, east and west. I am giving all this land, as far as you can see, to you and your descendants as a permanent possession. And I will give you so many descendants that, like the dust of the earth, they cannot be counted!" (verses 14-16).

Years later—still with no child of his own—Abram wondered if perhaps his chief servant, Eliezer, would become his official heir. The Lord soothed the patriarch's fear.

The LORD said to him, "No, your servant will not be your heir, for you will have a son of your own who will be your heir." Then the LORD took Abram outside and said to him, "Look up into the sky and count the stars if you can. That's how many descendants you will have!" . . .

So the LORD made a covenant with Abram that day and said, "I have given this land to your descendants, all the way from the border of Egypt to the great Euphrates River—the land now occupied by the Kenites, Kenizzites, Kadmonites, Hittites, Perizzites, Rephaites, Amorites, Canaanites, Girgashites, and Jebusites."

GENESIS 15:4-6; 18-21

We don't like waiting, but that's when God does some of His best work on our souls. When I'm forced to wait on God's timing, I change. Sometimes I discover that my request was selfish—not part of God's agenda at all. Other times I find that my level of maturity could not yet bear the blessing God wanted me to enjoy; I had to grow up so I could handle it well. Very often, my circumstances needed to change, or the blessing would have become a burden.

As we see Abram's faith journey unfold, we'll see why he had to wait so long to receive God's promised blessings.

God promised a *personal* **unconditional blessing.** This included great wealth as well as personal protection. Later in the story, we're told that "Abram was very rich in livestock, silver, and gold" (Genesis 13:2). He was known for receiving many blessings from God, including "flocks of sheep and goats, herds of cattle, a fortune in silver and gold, and many male and female servants and camels and donkeys" (Genesis 24:35). The people of Canaan referred to him as "an honored prince among us" (Genesis 23:6).

This is a good place to pause and say God does not condemn the wealthy. God reserves the right to bless some with an abundance of money and material possessions, and not bless others in that way. That's His sovereign right. In our materialistic culture, we might accuse God of cruelty for withholding material blessing from some, but God's economy doesn't trade in our currency. Some of His most honored servants haven't had two shekels to rub together, including His own Son. He does promise, however, that temporal poverty for His sake will be richly rewarded in eternity (see Matthew 6:33; Mark 10:29-31).

We don't like waiting, but that's when God does some of His best work on our souls.

Abram never apologized for being rich. In fact, God used his riches in wonderful ways, as we will see later.

God promised an *international* unconditional blessing. On top of the national and the personal blessings, God heaped a blessing upon all of humanity: "All the families on earth will be blessed through you" (Genesis 12:3). This refers to all races and nationalities—the whole world. God would bring a blessing to all people through the descendants of Abram, the Hebrew nation.

In His grand plan to redeem the world from sin and evil, God built a nation founded upon one man's faith. This nation would be a "kingdom of priests and a holy nation" (Exodus 19:6, ESV), responsible for leading the ignorant, superstitious, idol-worshiping nations into a relationship with the one true Creator God. The Lord established the Hebrew people as "a light for the nations, to open the eyes that are blind" (Isaiah 42:6-7, ESV). He said, "I will make you a light to the Gentiles, and you will bring my salvation to the ends of the earth" (Isaiah 49:6). And to help them accomplish this great task, He situated Israel on a little land-bridge nestled between the expansive Arabian Desert and the vast Mediterranean Sea.

Anyone traveling between the great empires of the ancient world—Egypt, Assyria, and Babylon—had to pass through the land promised to Abram's descendants. If Israel remained faithful to their calling, merchants, armies, and vagabonds would see a blessed nation and ask, "Who is this incredible king who makes you so prosperous and secure?" And the Hebrew people could answer, "Our King is the God of Abram! Would you like to know Him?"

ABRAM'S HALFWAY OBEDIENCE	
Genesis 11:31–12:3	**Acts 7:2-4**
One day Terah took his son Abram, his daughter-in-law Sarai (his son Abram's wife), and his grandson Lot (his son Haran's child) and moved away from Ur of the Chaldeans. He was headed for the land of Canaan, but they stopped at Haran and settled there. Terah lived for 205 years and died while still in Haran. The LORD had said to Abram, "Leave your native country, your relatives, and your father's family, and go to the land that I will show you. I will make you into a great nation. I will bless you and make you famous, and you will be a blessing to others. I will bless those who bless you and curse those who treat you with contempt. All the families on earth will be blessed through you."	Our glorious God appeared to our ancestor Abraham in Mesopotamia before he settled in Haran. God told him, "Leave your native land and your relatives, and come into the land that I will show you." So Abraham left the land of the Chaldeans and lived in Haran until his father died. Then God brought him here to the land where you now live.

After spending much of his life—perhaps from birth—in Ur of the Chaldeans, Abram was instructed by God to "leave your native country, your relatives, and your father's family" and go to a place to be disclosed later. Sadly, he didn't respond with complete obedience; he obeyed only in part. When he left Ur, Abram brought along his father, Terah, and his nephew, Lot. And with them came their households and possessions.

Abram moved in the general direction of Canaan—the land God had promised him—but he traveled no farther than Haran. According to ancient inscriptions, the main trade routes from Damascus, Nineveh, and Carchemish converged in this city. Perhaps lured by material abundance and the opportunity to build wealth, Abram's caravan got sidetracked. More likely, however, another obstacle stood between Abram and complete obedience. The moon god, Sin, whom Abram's family worshiped, had two principle seats of worship: Ur of the Chaldeans and . . . (you guessed it) Haran.

It wouldn't be hard to imagine that Abram's father, a lifelong devotee of the moon god, couldn't tear himself away from the deity's sanctuary in Haran, known to the locals as "house of rejoicing." This is why the Lord instructed Abram to leave his family behind; He knew they would become a perpetual distraction from his calling. When Abram's father decided to linger in Haran, Abram should have bade his father farewell and pressed on to Canaan.

Abram also allowed his nephew, Lot, to tag along, possibly because he felt sorry for the younger man. Lot's father had died some years earlier (see Genesis 11:27-28), and he undoubtedly latched on to Abram for fatherly guidance. Conversely, Abram may have viewed Lot as his potential heir, having no son of his own. As the story progresses, however, Lot proves to be an even greater distraction than Abram's father. Life threatening, in fact.

YOUR DEVELOPING FAITH

Genesis 12:4 begins the story of Abram's seedling faith becoming a fully mature, fruit-bearing tree. I am comforted to see that God didn't void His covenant with Abram because he failed to obey fully. Fortunately for Abram—and for us—the Lord doesn't expect anyone to exercise perfect faith. Instead, He meets us where we are and then helps us cultivate increasingly more mature trust in Him. So I don't mind telling you that God isn't finished with me yet. He continues to stretch my faith muscle so that it will become ever stronger with use. And He's doing the same for you.

As you reflect on Abram's faltering start, let me encourage you to examine your own faith journey by asking yourself three penetrating questions.

1. Are you seeking God's will deliberately and passionately?

Of the seven deadly sins, sloth may be the most sinister of all. Deadly passivity can consume our lives, and before we know it, we have nothing to show for our years. But sloth isn't laziness. Sloth has little to do with inactivity. At its core, sloth is disconnecting from what should keep us passionate. Sloth is failing to follow the course set before us by God, failing to fulfill our divine purpose.

I challenge you to pray, "Lord, guide me into Your will, regardless of what change is necessary, regardless of where I must go or what I must do. I want You to know, Lord, I'm available. And I don't want to live outside Your will." Then be prepared for some uncomfortable answers to your prayer. Faith rarely involves easy choices.

Early in my ministry, several years after I had graduated from seminary, I took a pastorate in a suburb of Boston. Within eighteen months, I realized I was not a good fit at that church. I had sincerely thought this would be my place of ministry for years to come. Furthermore, that little church had spent $1,600 to move my family and me—a small fortune in the mid-1960s. I felt so embarrassed about the possibility of leaving only a couple of years after arriving. I kept saying, "Lord, I want to do Your will, but I don't think this is where I'm supposed to be."

Finally, I talked it over with Cynthia, and she agreed. But we were young and inexperienced; we didn't know what to do. What does a pastor do when he realizes he's not where the Lord wants him? There was nothing wrong with the church and they loved me, but I couldn't shake a sense of restlessness that became increasingly more distracting and burdensome.

I'll never forget visiting Tom, the chair of the elders. He ran a tuxedo shop, and I met him at his store. We walked behind the curtain and sat down in the back room. He said, "What's goin' on?"

Tears filled my eyes. I felt embarrassed and hated to break the news. "Tom, I've got to tell you, I don't think I ought to be here."

Naturally, he asked what anyone would ask. "What's wrong?"

"Nothing," I said.

"Nothing's wrong, and you don't think you ought to be here?"

"Right."

"Where do you want to go?"

"I don't know, Tom. I just know I can't stay here."

I'll never forget his gracious response—some of the most wonderful words I'd ever heard. "Chuck, if the Lord doesn't want you here, then we don't either."

He could have said, "Well, you know we spent a lot of money moving you here. We worked hard to set you up in a house. We even put up new wallpaper for you. We've gone to a lot of trouble, and this is how you thank us?" There was none of that shaming stuff. He joined me in submitting to God's leading, even though it didn't make a lot of sense.

That leads us to the second question.

2. If God were to have you leave your comfort zone to take on the challenges of the unfamiliar, how would you respond?

Trusting in God rarely involves easy choices. If every missionary looked for comfort or convenience or familiarity, missions would collapse overnight. Ministries would fold, and charities would close up shop. Every choice to follow God's leading involves sacrifice—at least the sacrifice of our own desires. Do you trust the Lord's character enough to obey Him without having all the details worked out? Are you willing to accept a short-term loss in order to receive divine blessings you cannot yet see?

3. Are you making obedience too complicated?
If you're discussing your decision with too many people or talking in endless circles, you're making obedience complicated. You're probably falling into one of the following traps:

> - You're hoping someone will give you a compelling reason to do something other than what you know in your heart to be God's will.
> - You're hoping to find a way to obey without having to face hardship and sacrifice.
> - You don't like risk, and you're hoping that God will change His mind if you delay making the decision long enough.
> - You're hoping that by talking and waiting, you'll feel good about the decision before having to commit.
> - You haven't yet accepted that there's no such thing as a decision without at least some negative consequences.

If you know what God wants you to do, obedience isn't complicated. It may be difficult, but it's not complicated. Stop hoping it will be easy, and give up the search for alternatives. Don't wait any longer for all the details to be worked out. The Lord has given you an opportunity to grow in faith. He wants you to trust in His faithful care and rest in His unfaltering power. The time to obey has come. Now . . .

Go!

Online Discussion *guide*

TAKE *your* TYNDALE READING EXPERIENCE *to the* NEXT LEVEL

A FREE discussion guide for this book is available at bookclubhub.net, perfect for sparking conversations in your book group or for digging deeper into the text on your own.

www.bookclubhub.net

You'll also find free discussion guides for other Tyndale books, e-newsletters, e-mail devotionals, virtual book tours, and more!

TWELVE TRIBES OF ISRAEL

Legend:
- • City
- ○ City of refuge
- ★ Capital city (foreign territory)
- ▲ Mountain peak

TYRE
ARAM
Sidon
Damascus ★
Mt. Hermon ▲
Litani R.
Abana R.
Ijon
Tyre
Dan
Kedesh ○
Lake Hula
EAST MANASSEH
Rehob
Abdon
Hazor
Merom
ASHER
NAPHTALI
Acco
Cabul
Capernaum
Sea of Galilee
Golan ○
Ashtaroth
Mediterranean Sea
(Great Sea)
Rimmon
Hannathon
Mt. Carmel ▲
Kishon R.
ZEBULUN
Daberath
Sarid
Mt. Tabor ▲
Yarmuk R.
Jokneam
Dor
Megiddo
Jezreel
Mt. Moreh ▲
ISSACHAR
Edrei
Taanach
Mt. Gilboa ▲
Beth-shan
Ramoth-gilead ○
Ibleam
En-gannim
Jordan R.
Jabesh-gilead
EASTERN DESERT
Dothan
WEST MANASSEH
Socoh
Samaria
Tirzah
Mt. Ebal ▲
Mt. Gerizim ○ Shechem
Succoth
Mahanaim Penuel
Jabbok R.
AMMON
Gath-rimmon
Aphek
Tappuah
Yarkon R.
Joppa
Shiloh
GAD
EPHRAIM
DAN
Bethel
Jazer
Rabbah (Amman) ★
Beth-horon
Mizpah
Gilgal
Acacia Grove
Gezer
Aijalon
BENJAMIN
Gibeon
Jericho
Heshbon
Gibbethon
Timnah
Kiriath-jearim
Jerusalem
Mt. Nebo ▲
Bezer ○
Ekron
Beth-shemesh
Ashdod
Gath
Bethlehem
Medeba
Ashkelon
Mareshah
REUBEN
Kedemoth
Lachish
Hebron ○
Jahaz
Gaza
Juttah
En-gedi
Dibon
JUDAH
Debir
Eshtemoa
Dead Sea (Salt Sea)
Aroer
Gerar
Ziklag
Arnon R.
Sharuhen
Arad
MOAB
Beersheba
Hormah
Kir-hareseth ★
SIMEON
Zoar
Zered Brook
ARABAH
Brook of Egypt
Besor Brook
Tamar
EDOM
Bozrah ★

Scale:
0   10   20 Miles
0   10   20 Kilometers

Old Testament Scrolls

LAW
Genesis · Exodus · Leviticus · Numbers · Deuteronomy

HISTORY
Joshua · Judges · Ruth · 1 & 2 Samuel · 1 & 2 Kings · 1 & 2 Chronicles · Ezra · Nehemiah · Esther

POETRY
Job · Psalms · Proverbs · Ecclesiastes · Song of Solomon

MAJOR PROPHETS
Isaiah · Jeremiah · Lamentations · Ezekiel · Daniel

MINOR PROPHETS
Hosea · Joel · Amos · Obadiah · Jonah · Micah · Nahum · Habakkuk · Zephaniah · Haggai · Zechariah · Malachi

New Testament Scrolls

GOSPELS
Matthew · Mark · Luke · John

HISTORY
Acts

PAUL'S LETTERS
Romans · 1 & 2 Corinthians · Galatians · Ephesians · Philippians · Colossians · 1 & 2 Thessalonians · 1 & 2 Timothy · Titus · Philemon

GENERAL LETTERS
Hebrews · James · 1 & 2 Peter · 1, 2 & 3 John · Jude

PROPHECY
Revelation

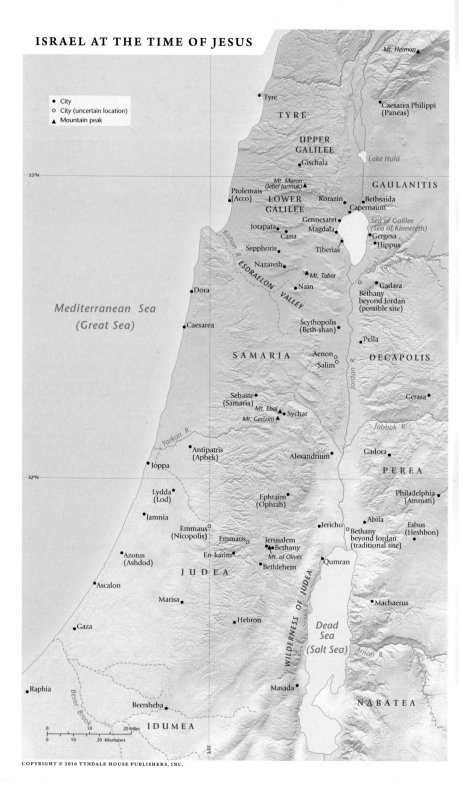

ISRAEL AT THE TIME OF JESUS

- City
- ○ City (uncertain location)
- ▲ Mountain peak

Mt. Hermon ▲

Tyre

TYRE

Caesarea Philippi (Paneas)

UPPER GALILEE

Gischala

Lake Hula

33°N

Mt. Meron (Jebel Jarmuk) ▲

GAULANITIS

Ptolemais (Acco)

LOWER GALILEE

Korazin

Bethsaida

Capernaum

Gennesaret

Jotapata

Sea of Galilee (Sea of Kinnereth)

Cana

Magdala

Gergesa

Sepphoris

Hippus

Tiberias

Nazareth

KISHON R.

ESDRAELON VALLEY

Mt. Tabor ▲

Nain

Yarmuk R.

Dora

Gadara

Bethany beyond Jordan (possible site)

Mediterranean Sea (Great Sea)

Caesarea

Scythopolis (Beth-shan)

Pella

SAMARIA

Aenon ○

Salim ○

DECAPOLIS

Jordan R.

Gerasa

Sebaste (Samaria)

Jabbok R.

Mt. Ebal ▲

Sychar

Mt. Gerizim ▲

Yarkon R.

Antipatris (Aphek)

Alexandrium

Gadora

Joppa

PEREA

32°N

Lydda (Lod)

Ephraim (Ophrah)

Philadelphia (Amman)

Jamnia

Abila

Emmaus (Nicopolis) ○

Esbus (Heshbon)

Emmaus ○

Jericho

Azotus (Ashdod)

En-karim

Jerusalem

Bethany

Bethany beyond Jordan (traditional site)

Mt. of Olives

Bethlehem

Qumran

JUDEA

Ascalon

Marisa

WILDERNESS OF JUDEA

Hebron

Machaerus

Gaza

Dead Sea (Salt Sea)

Arnon R.

Raphia

Besor Brook

Masada

NABATEA

Beersheba

IDUMEA

0   10   20 Miles

0   10   20 Kilometers

35°E

COPYRIGHT © 2016 TYNDALE HOUSE PUBLISHERS, INC.